TO:

_____

FROM:

_____

HAPPINESS

IS A

WARM PUPPY

BY
CHARLES M. SCHULZ

PENGUIN WORKSHOP
An Imprint of Penguin Random House LLC, New York

© 1962 Peanuts Worldwide LLC. All rights reserved. This edition published in 2019 by Penguin Workshop, an imprint of Penguin Random House LLC, New York. PENGUIN and PENGUIN WORKSHOP are trademarks of Penguin Books Ltd, and the W colophon is a registered trademark of Penguin Random House LLC. Manufactured in China.

Visit us online at www.penguinrandomhouse.com.

Library of Congress Cataloging-in-Publication Data is available upon request.

ISBN 9781524789954

10 9 8 7 6 5 4 3 2

HAPPINESS

IS A

WARM PUPPY

Happiness is a thumb and a blanket.

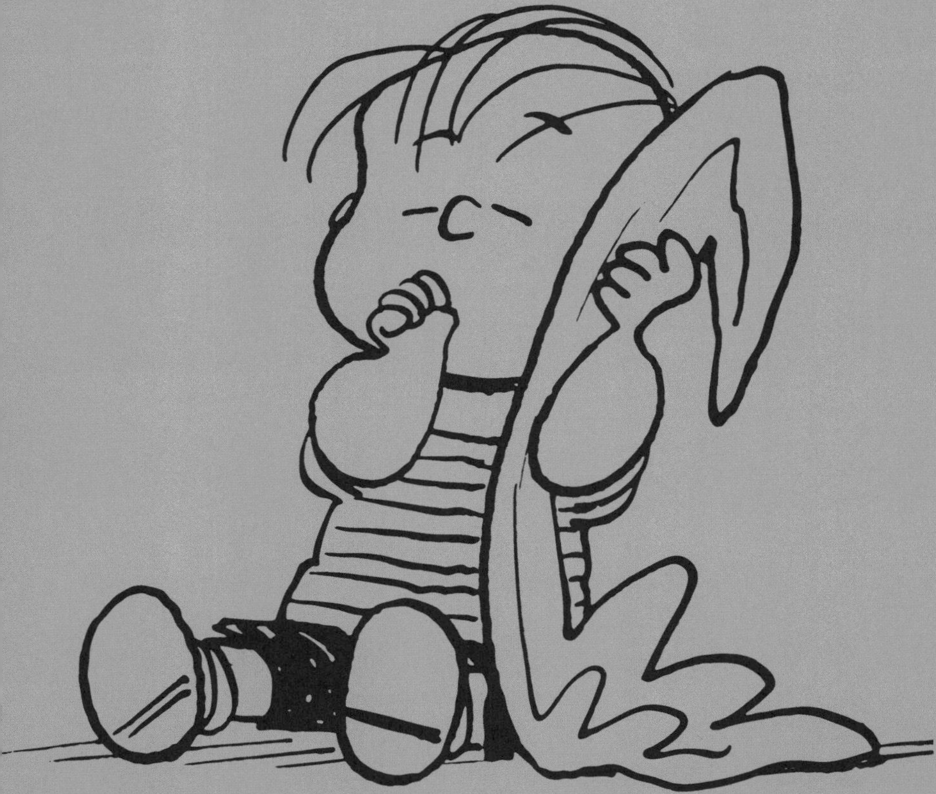

Happiness is an umbrella and a new raincoat.

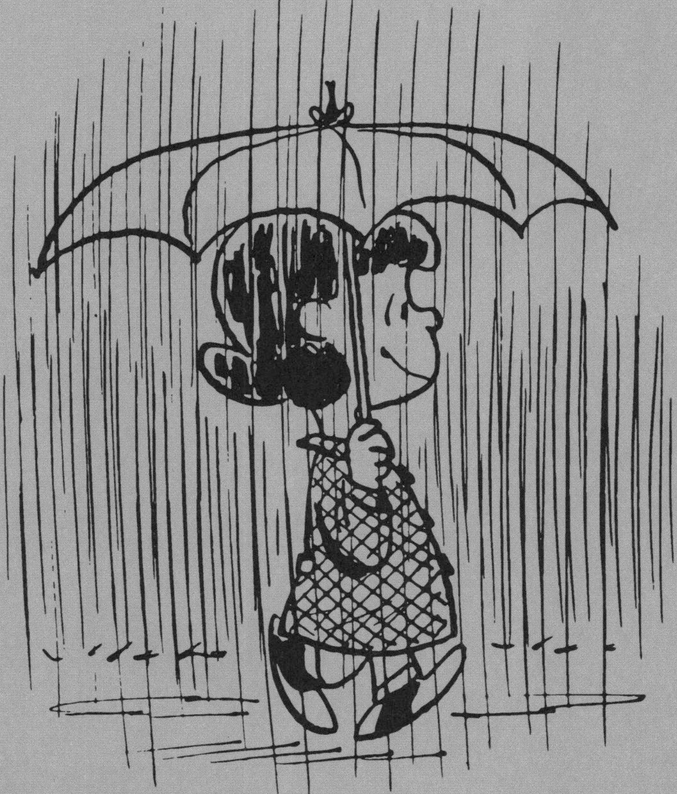

Happiness is a pile of leaves.

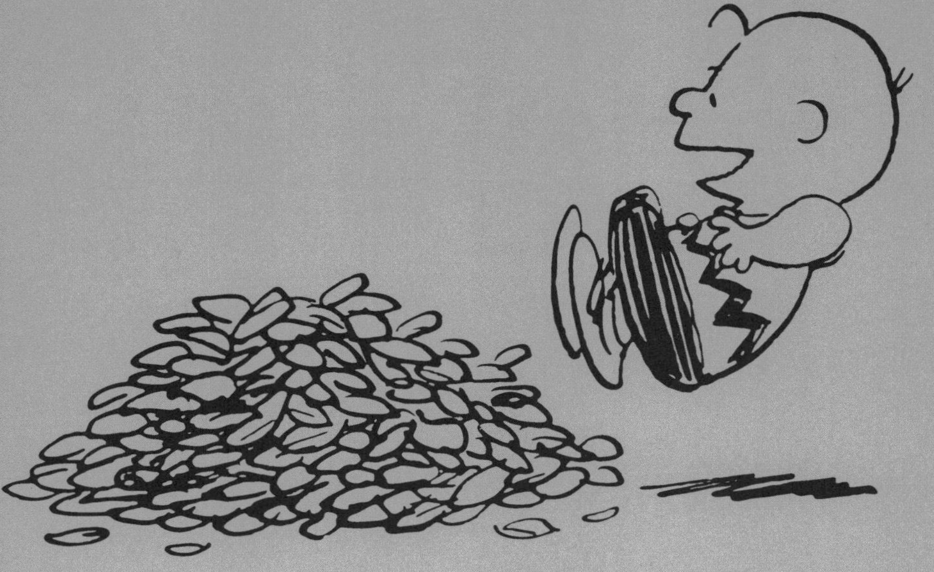

Happiness is a warm puppy.

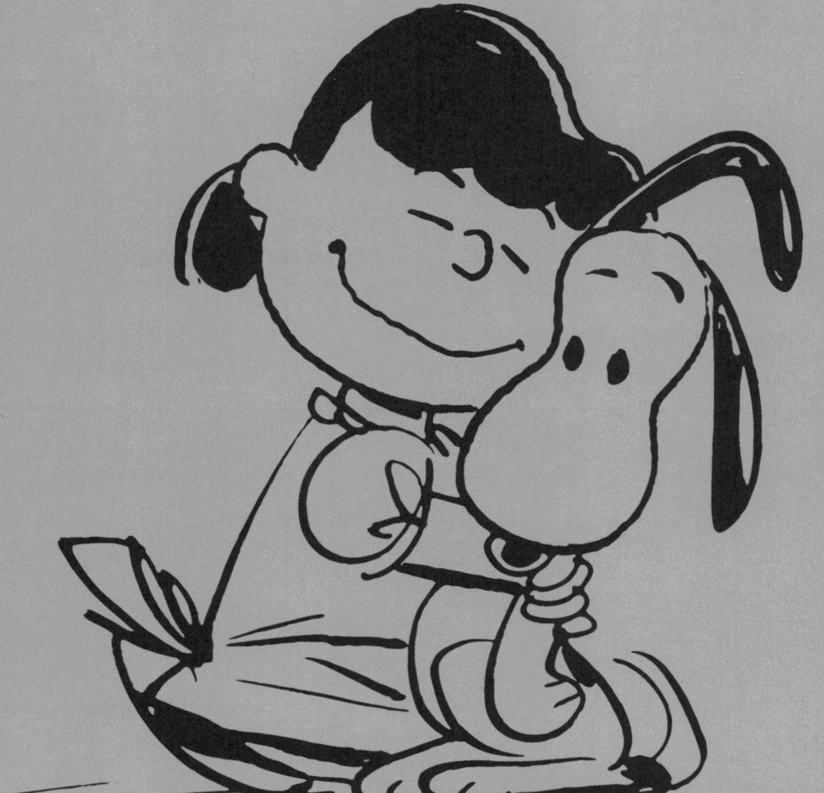

Happiness
is
an
"A"
on your
spelling test.

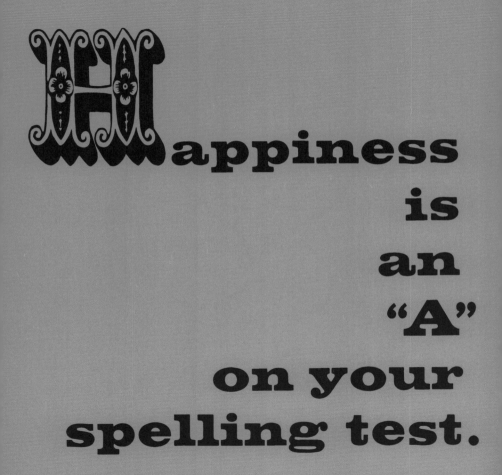

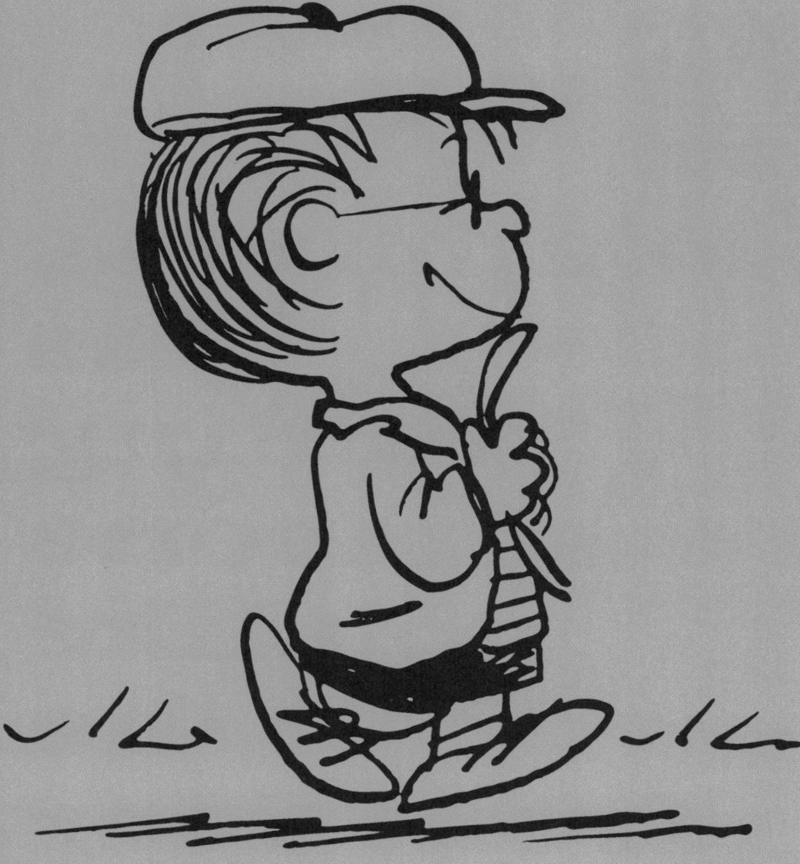

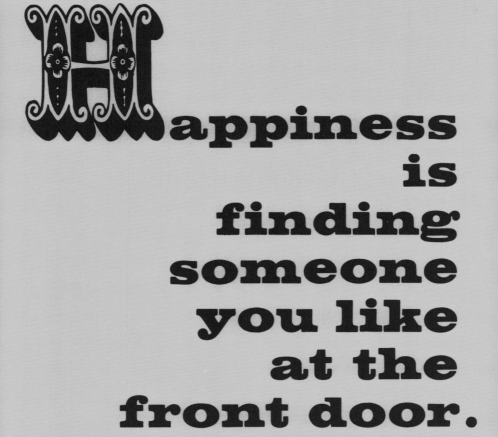

Happiness
is
finding
someone
you like
at the
front door.

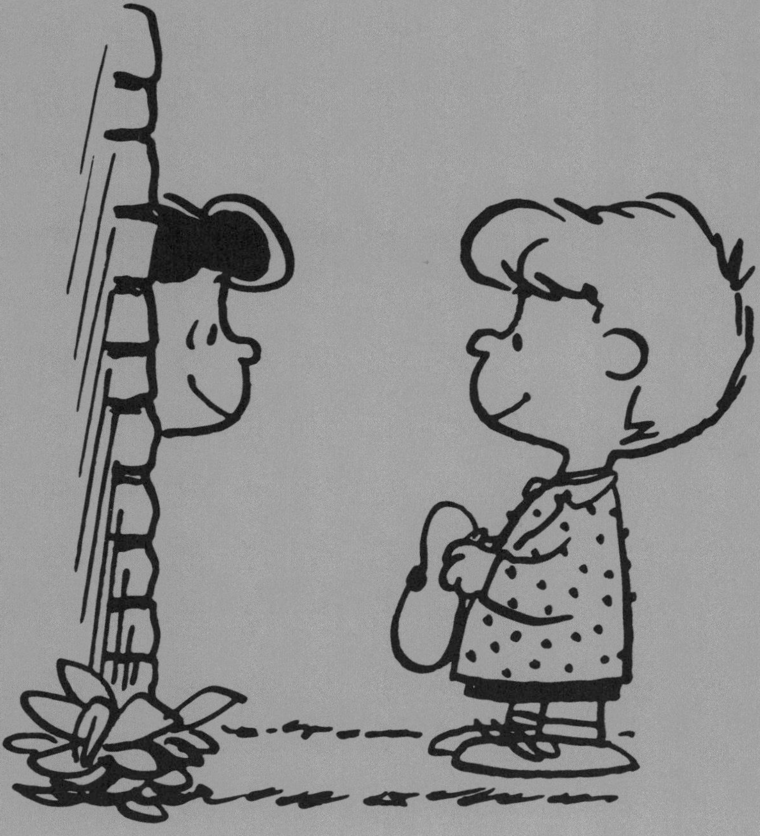

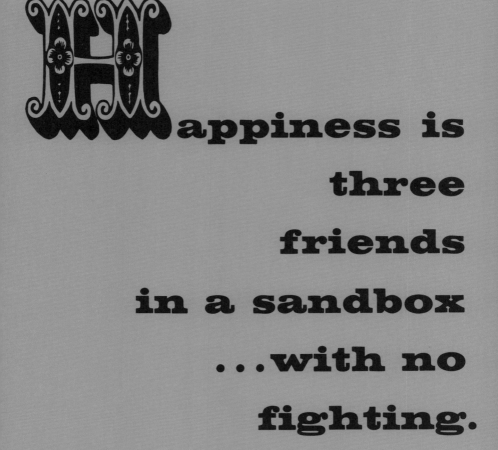

Happiness is three friends in a sandbox ...with no fighting.

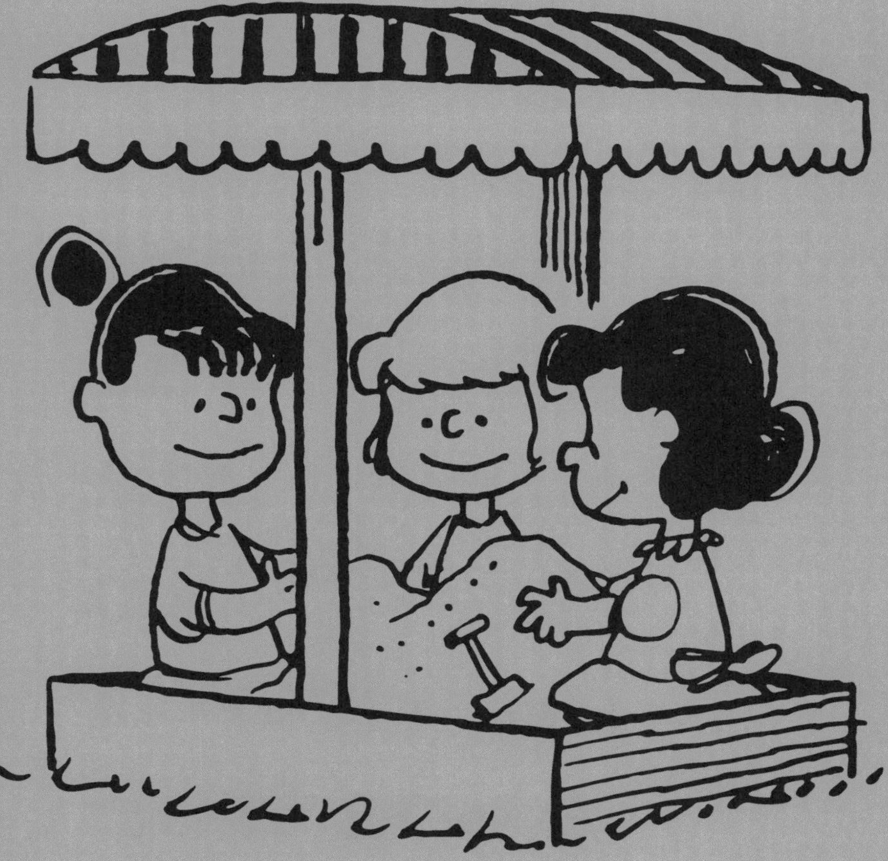

Happiness is sleeping in your own bed.

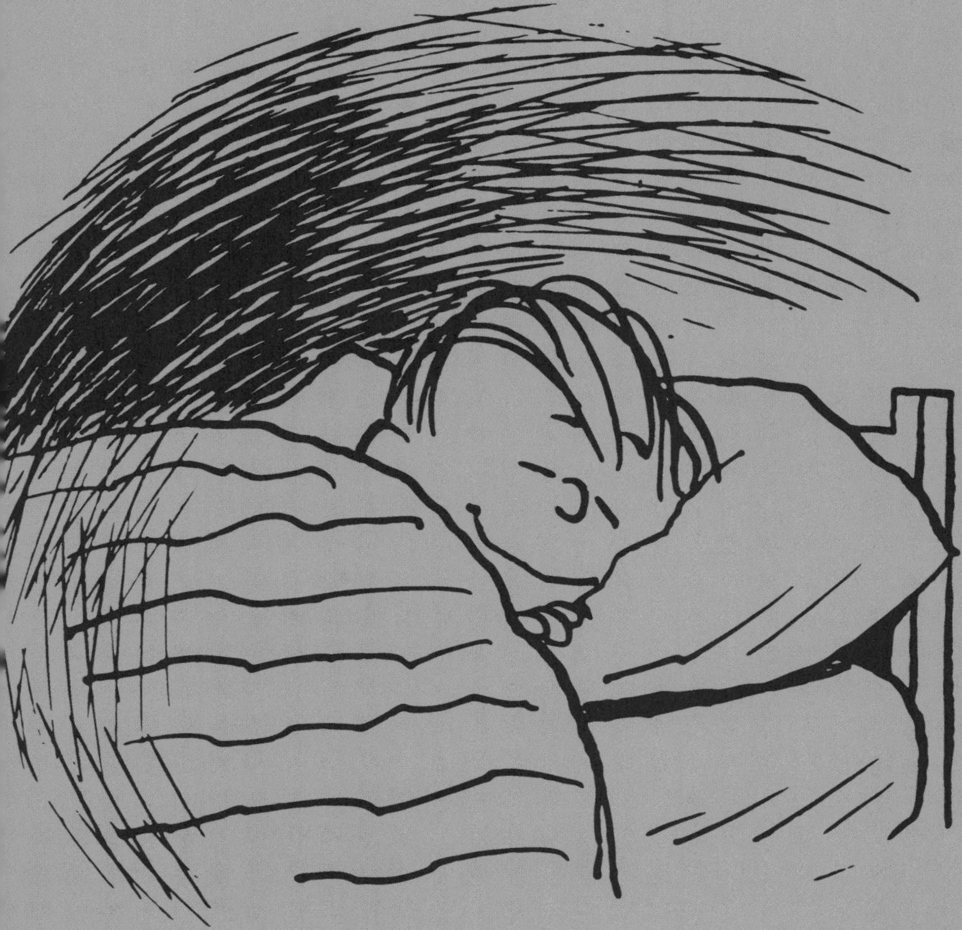

Happiness

is

a

chain

of

paper clips.

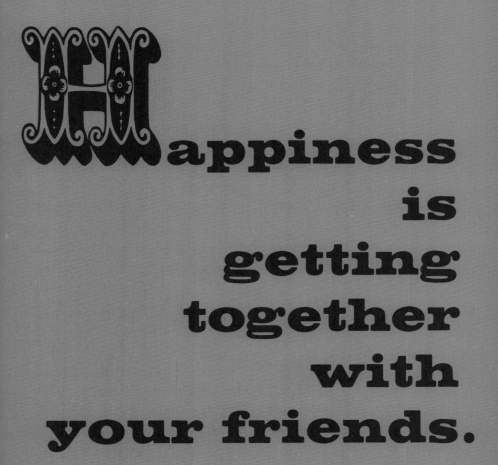

Happiness is getting together with your friends.

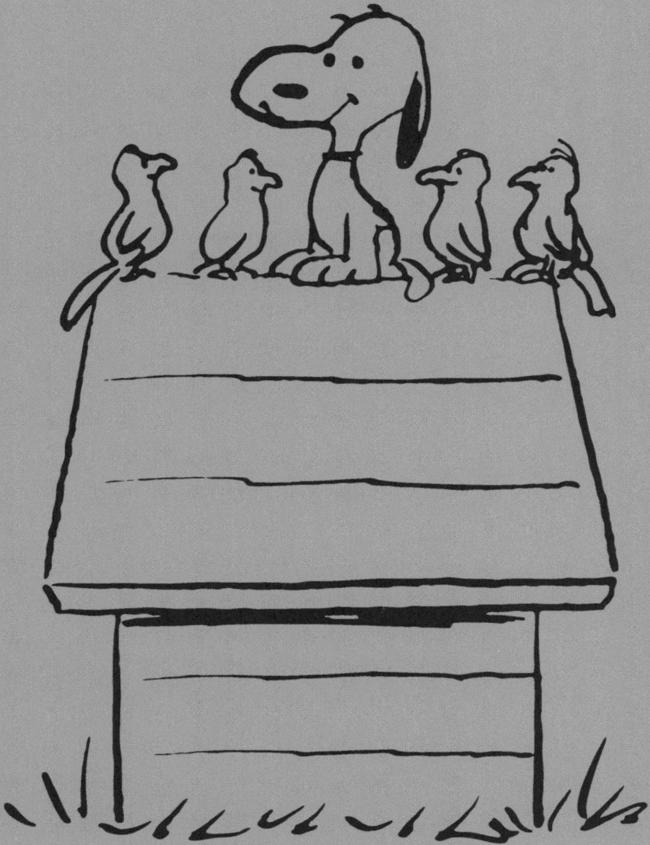

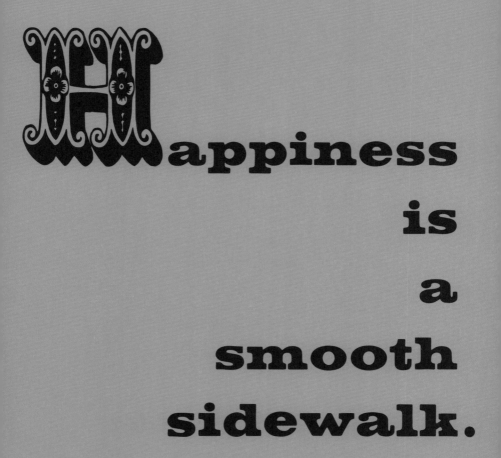

Happiness is a smooth sidewalk.

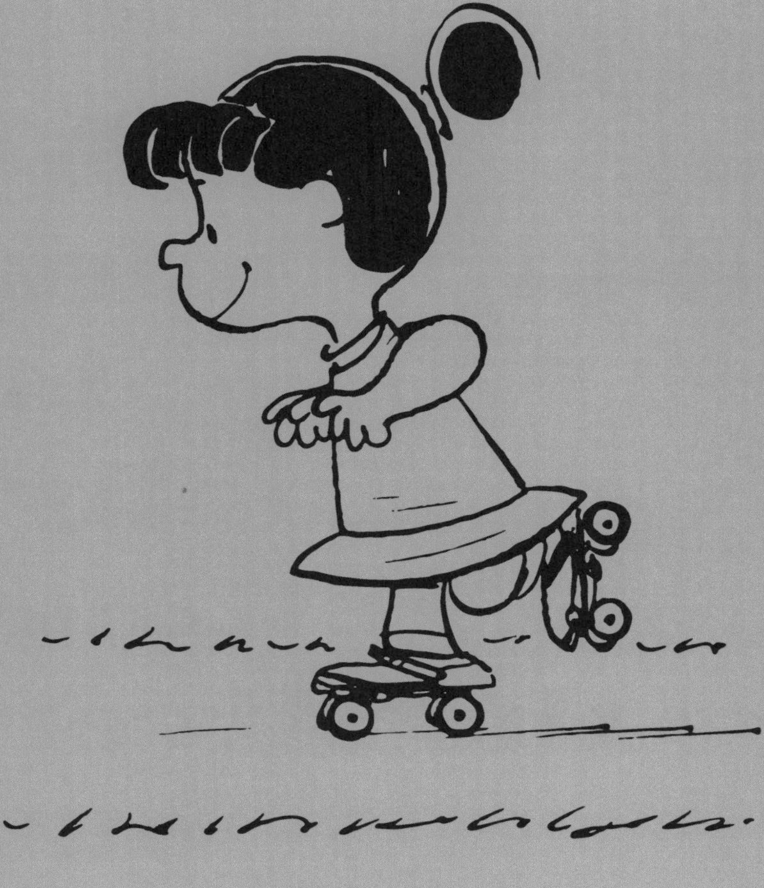

Happiness is finally getting the sliver out.

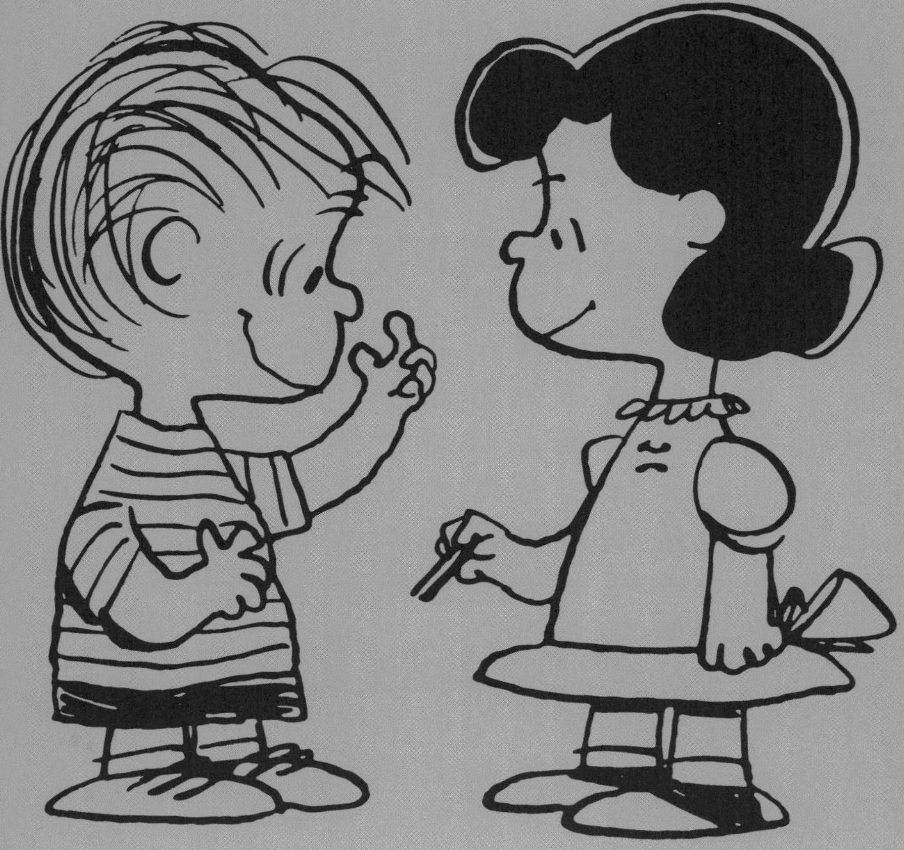

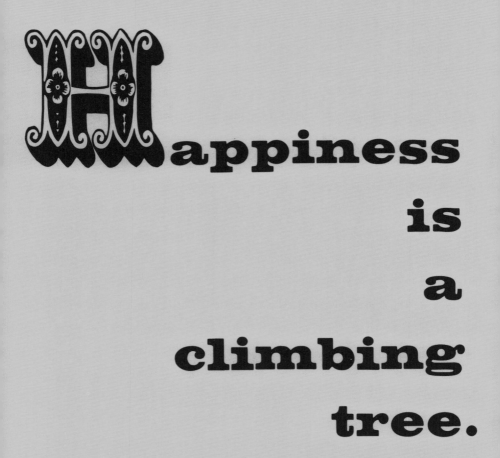

Happiness is a climbing tree.

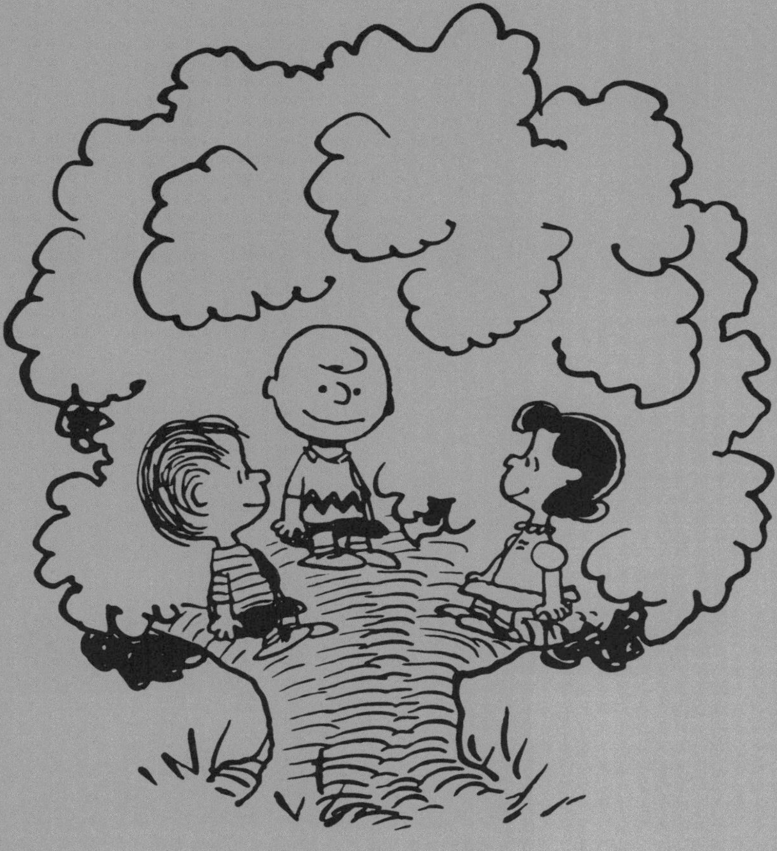

Happiness is lots of candles.

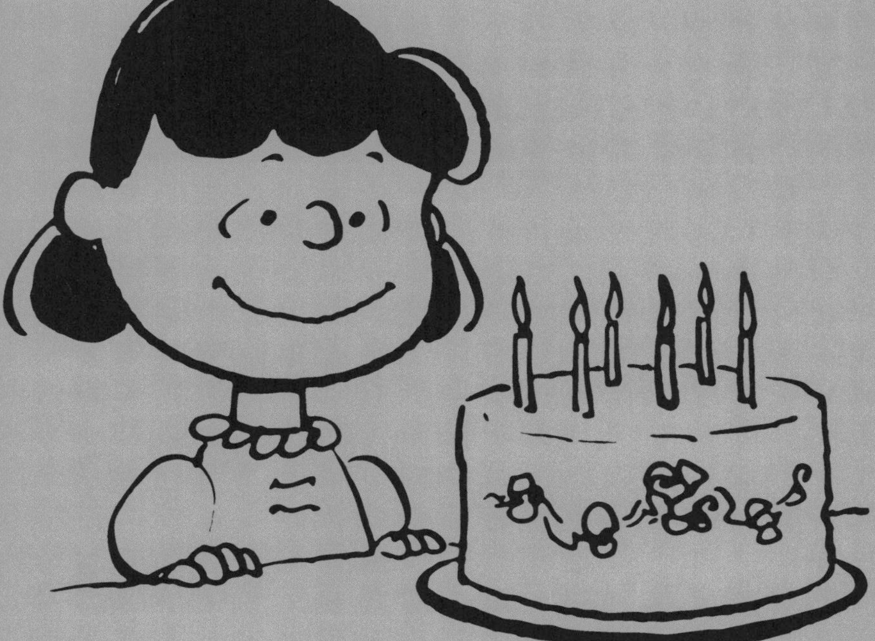

Happiness is being able to reach the doorknob.

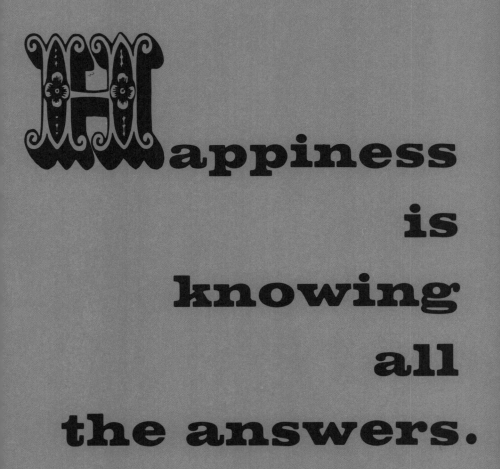

Happiness is knowing all the answers.

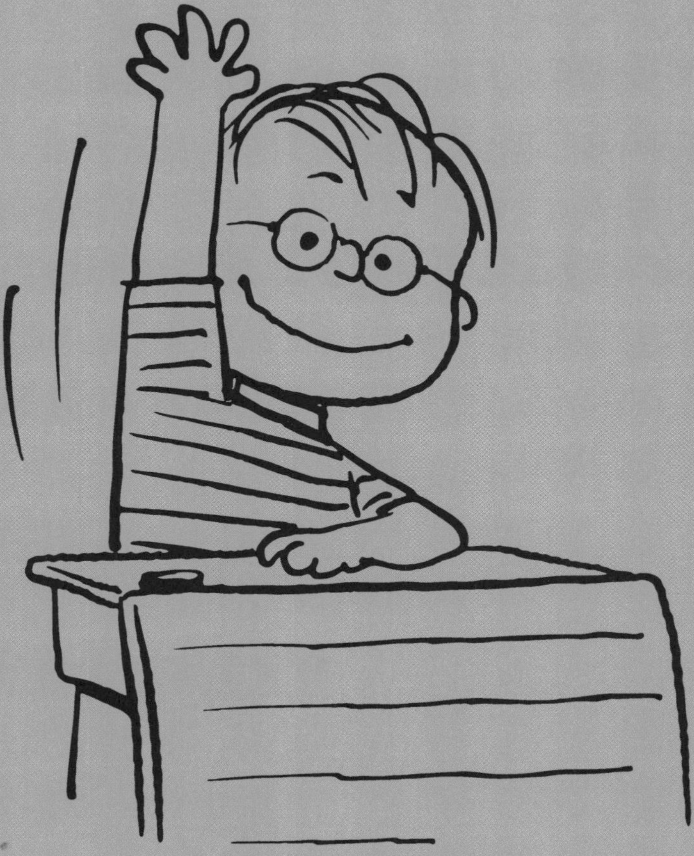

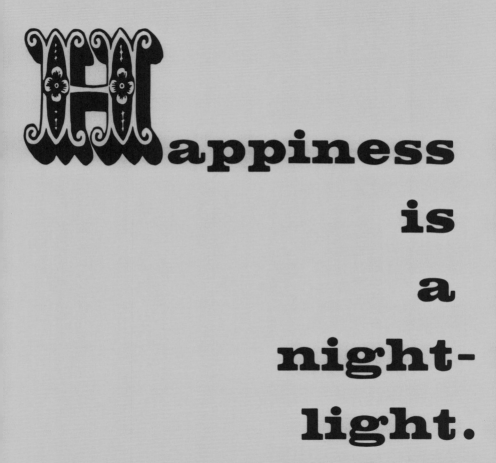

Happiness is a night-light.

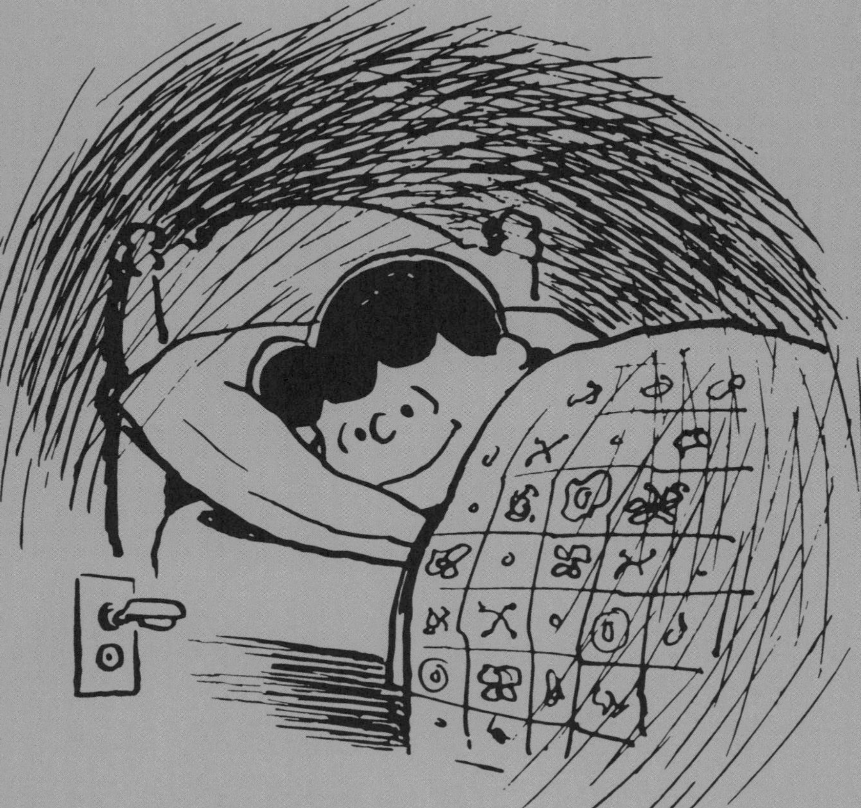

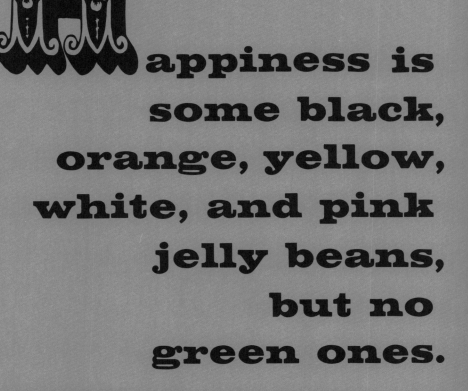

Happiness is some black, orange, yellow, white, and pink jelly beans, but no green ones.

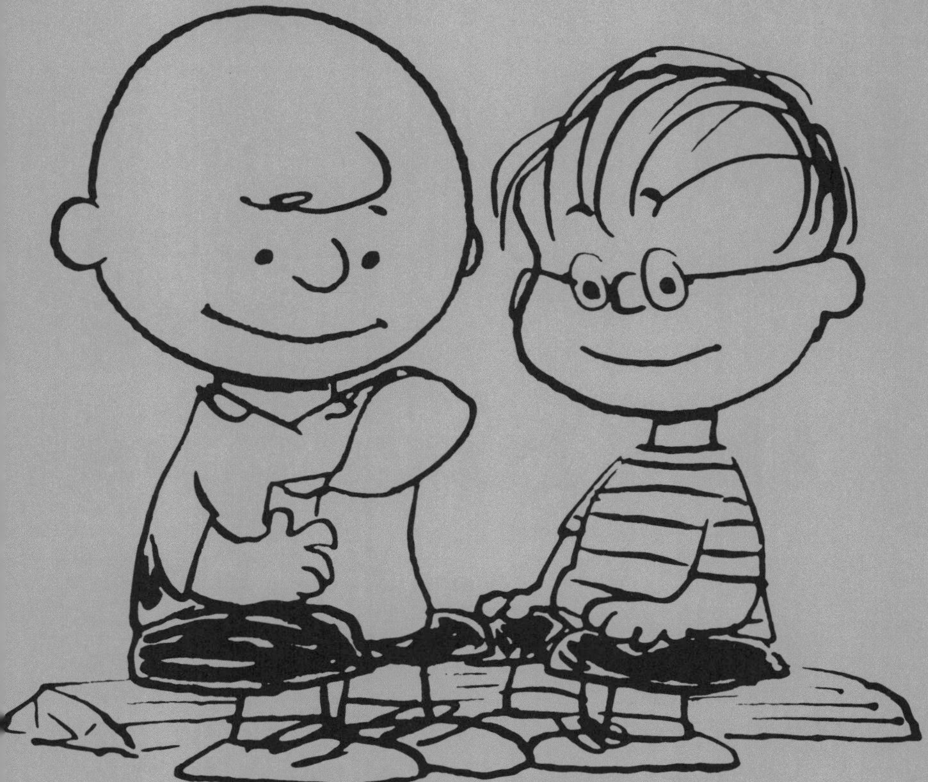

Happiness is the hiccups ...after they've gone away.

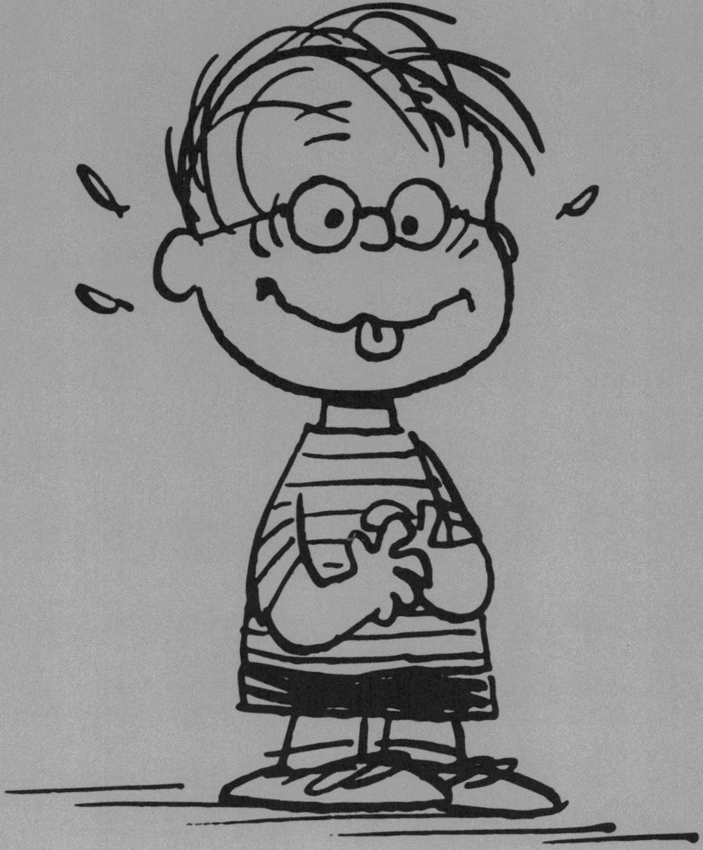

appiness
is
a
good
old-fashioned
game of
hide-and-seek.

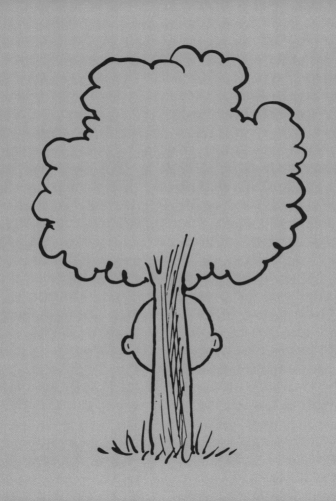

appiness

is

a

fuzzy

sweater.

Happiness is a bread-and-butter sandwich folded over.

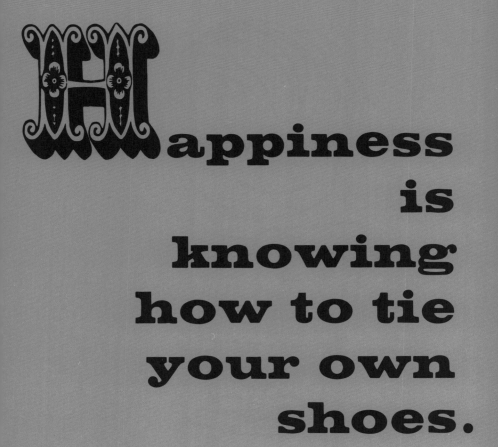

Happiness is knowing how to tie your own shoes.

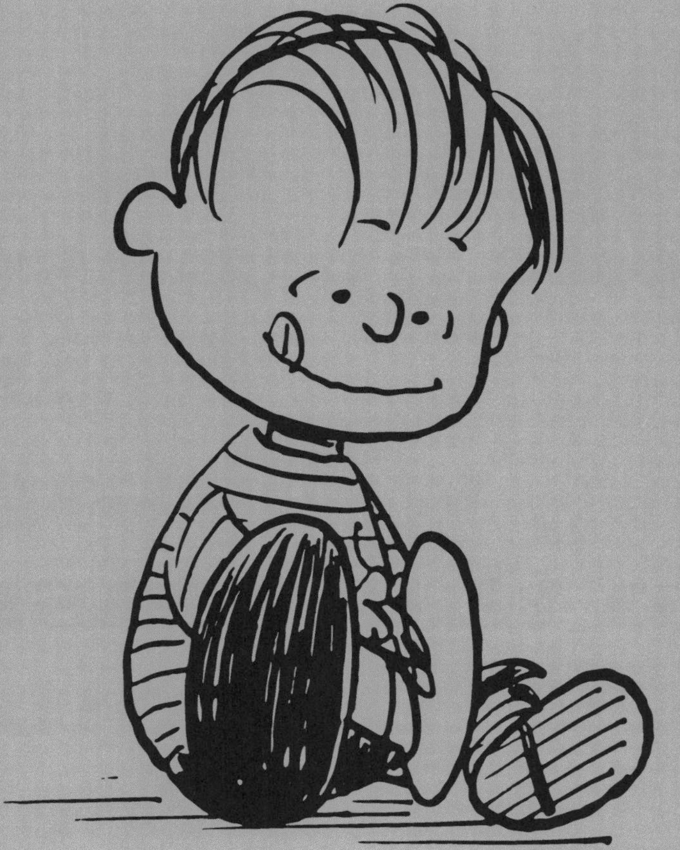

Happiness is walking in the grass in your bare feet.

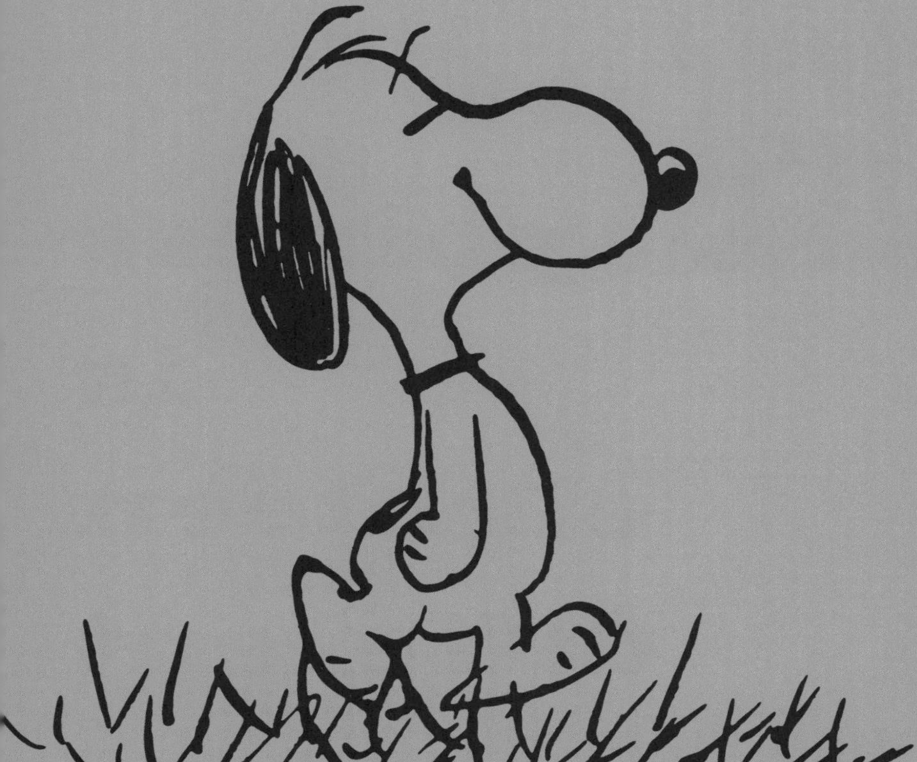

Happiness is eighteen different colors.

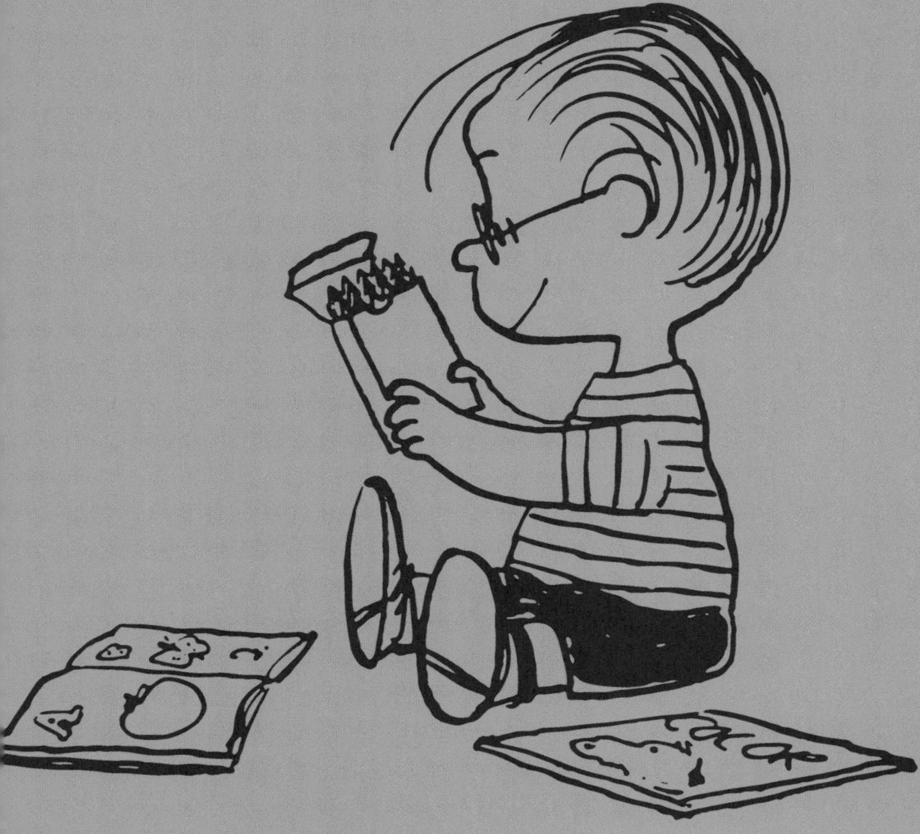

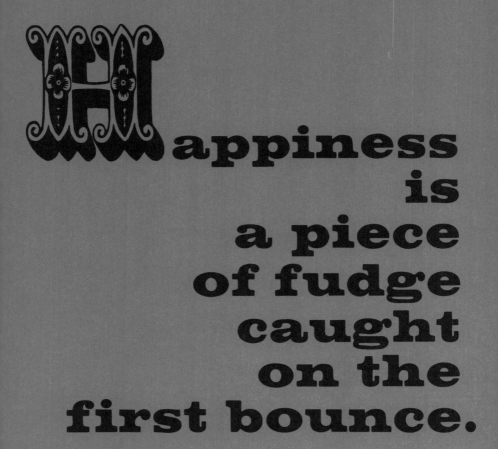

Happiness
is
a piece
of fudge
caught
on the
first bounce.

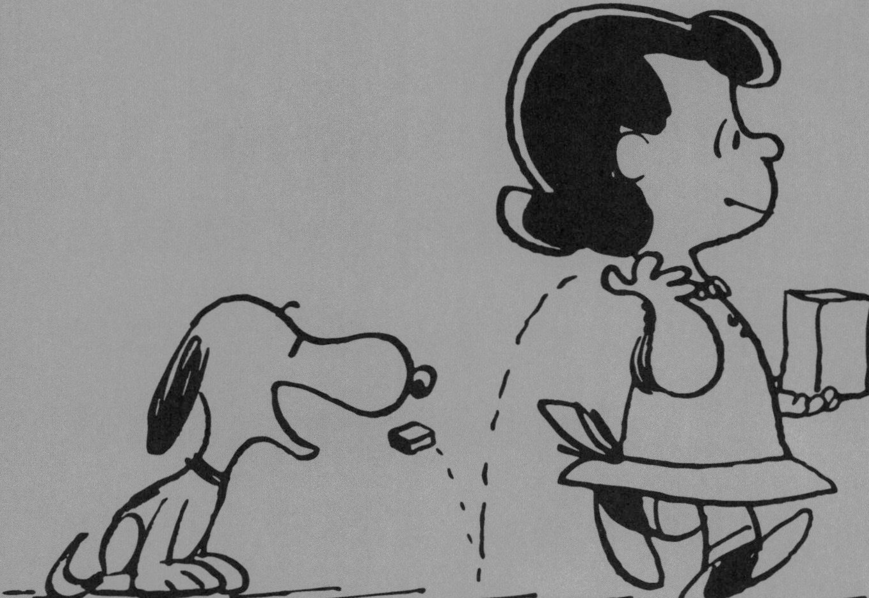

Happiness is finding the little piece with the pink edge and part of the sky and the top of the sailboat.

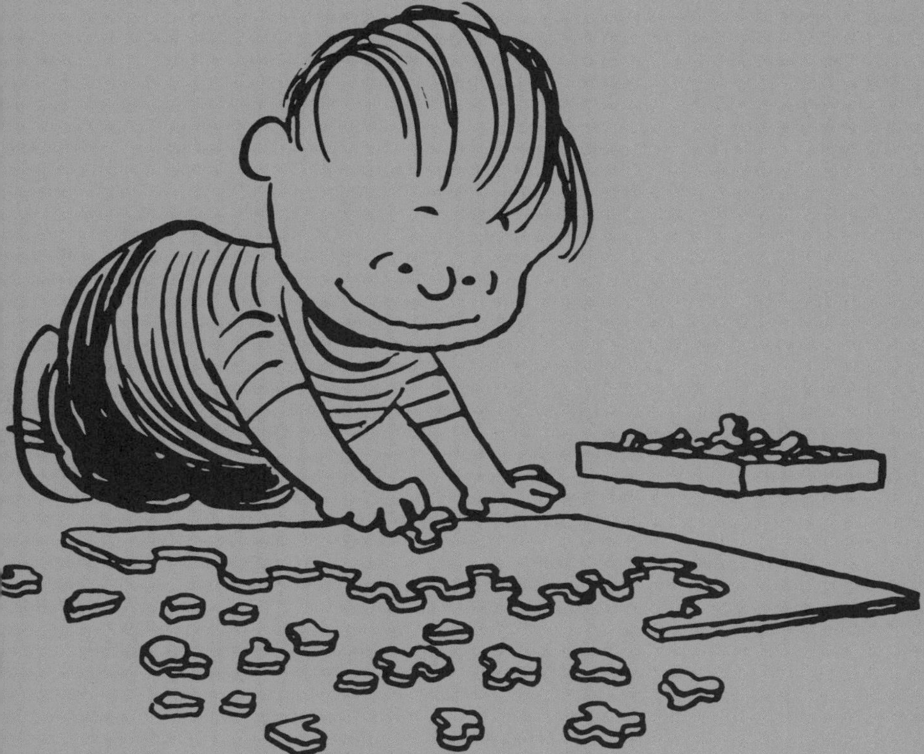

Happiness is finding out you're not so dumb after all.

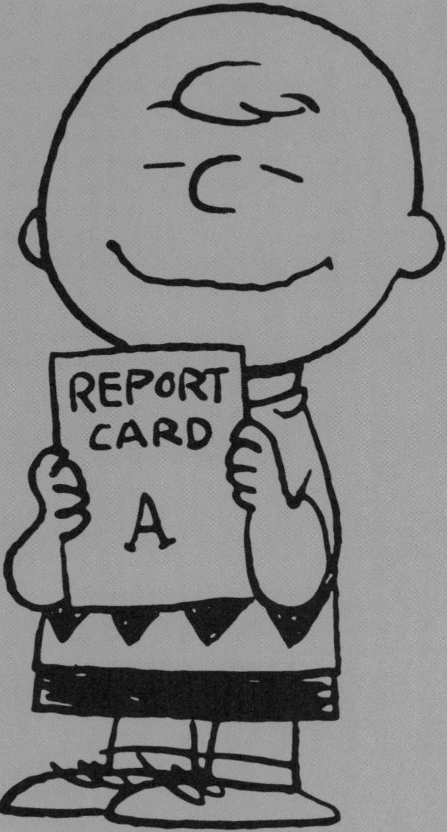
REPORT
CARD
A

Happiness is thirty-five cents for the movie, fifteen cents for popcorn, and a nickel for a candy bar.

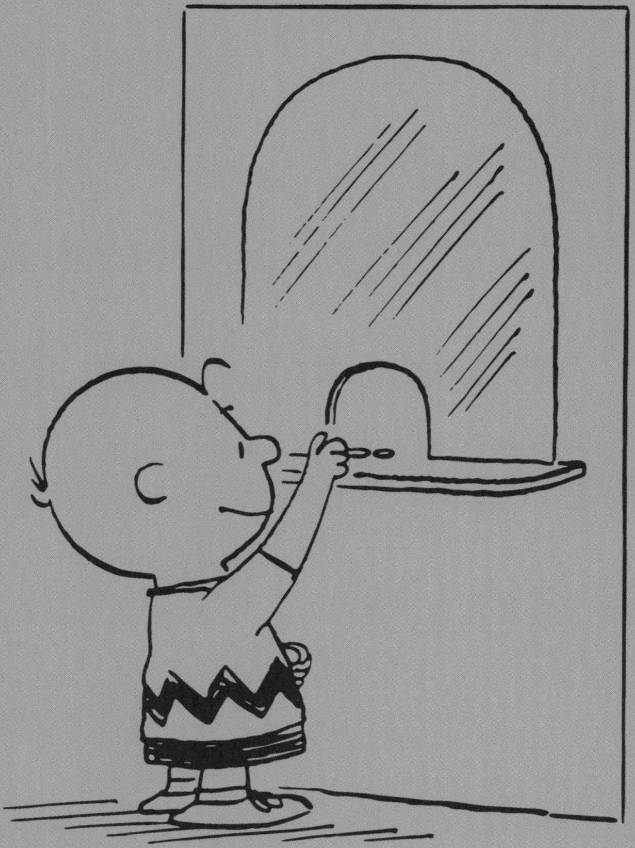

Happiness is one thing to one person and another thing to another person.

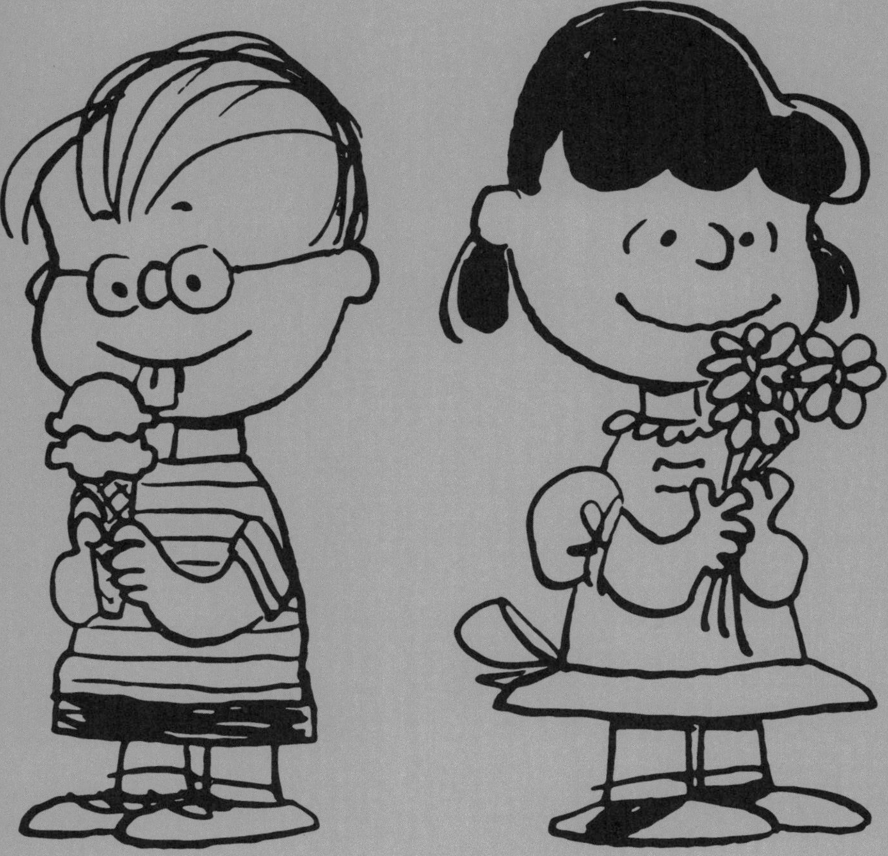

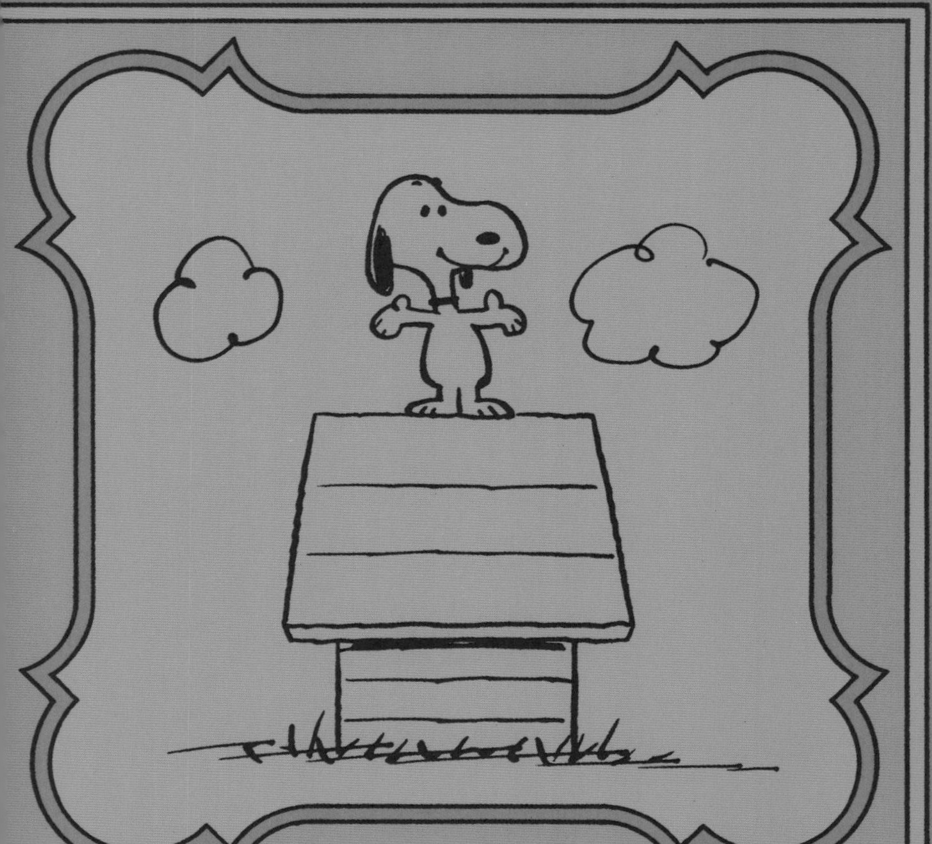

Love is
the
whole
world

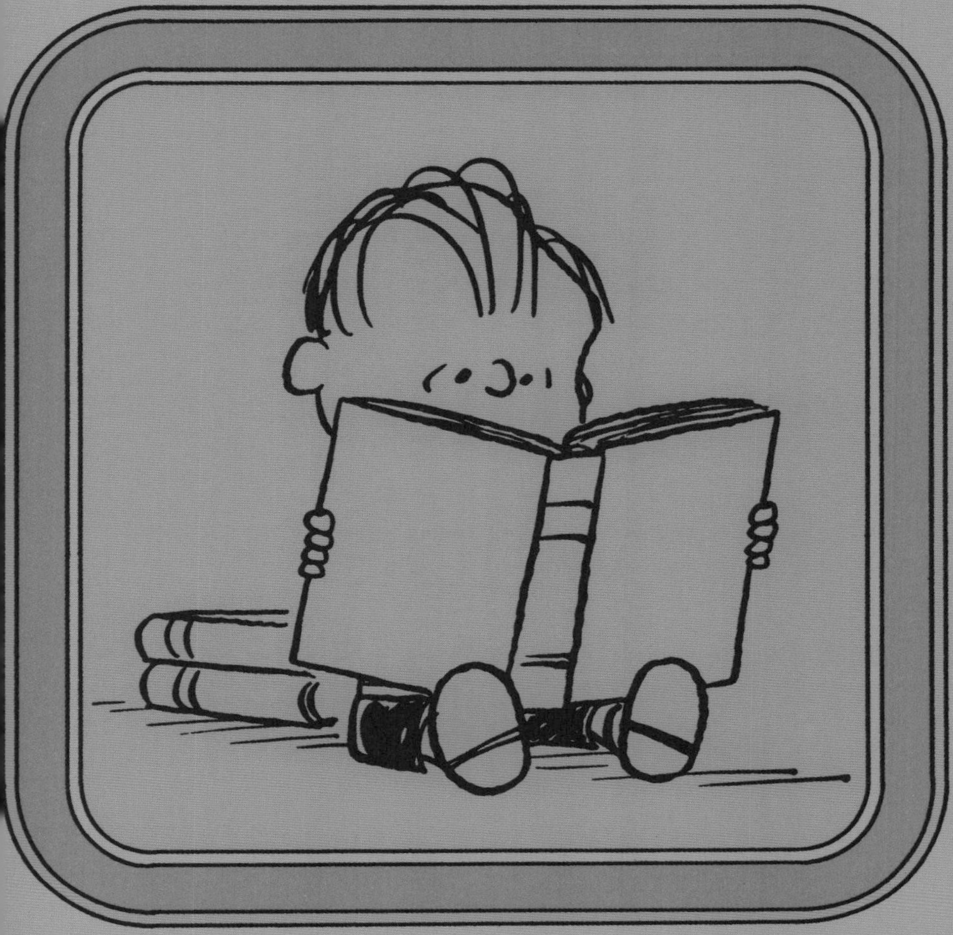

Love is
liking
ideas

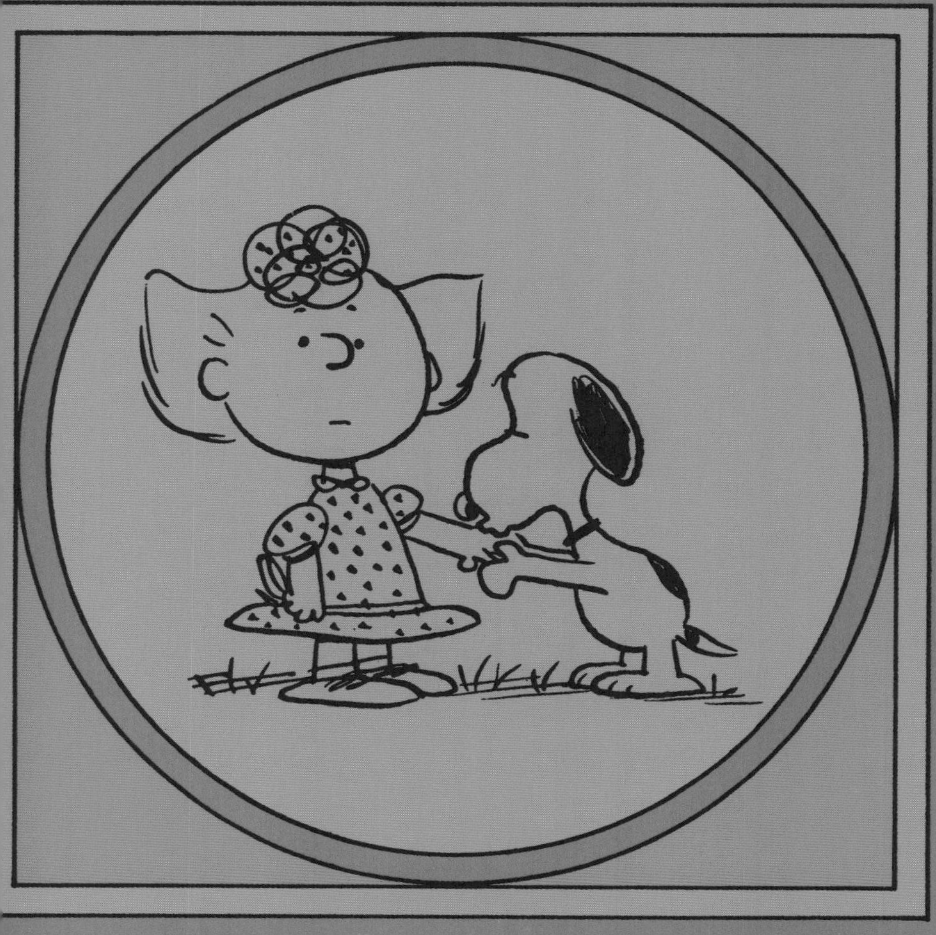

Love is
liking
people

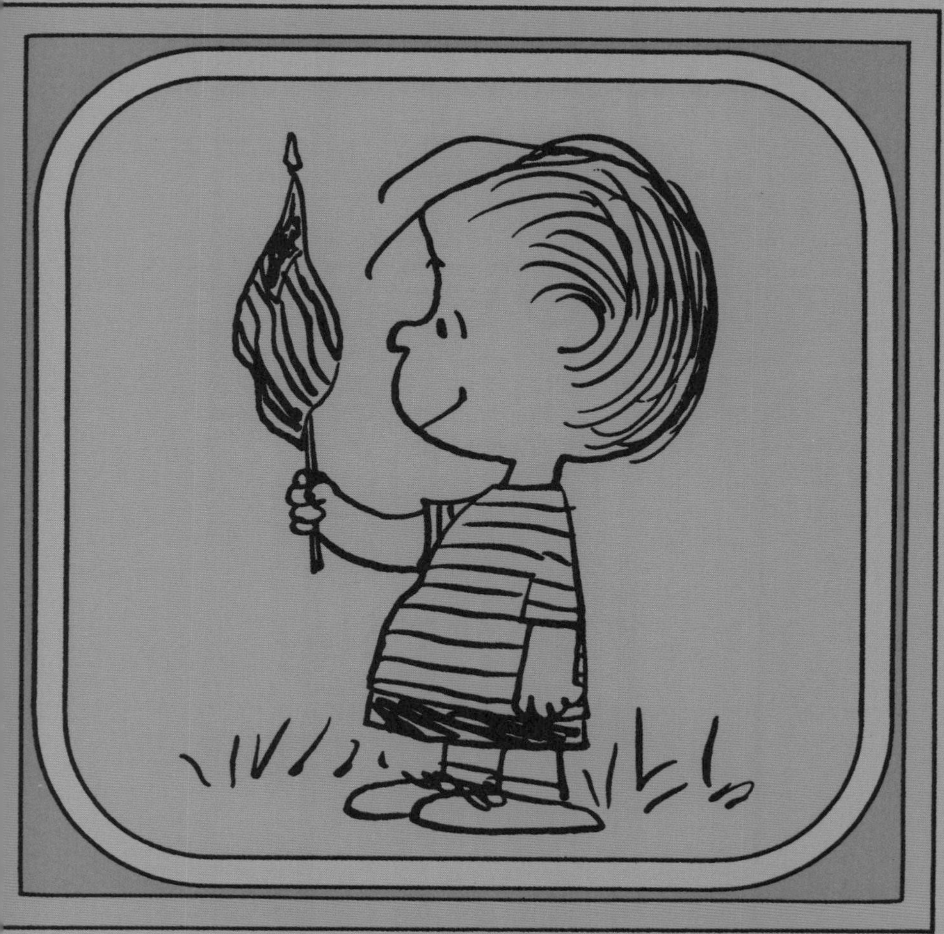

Love

is a

flag

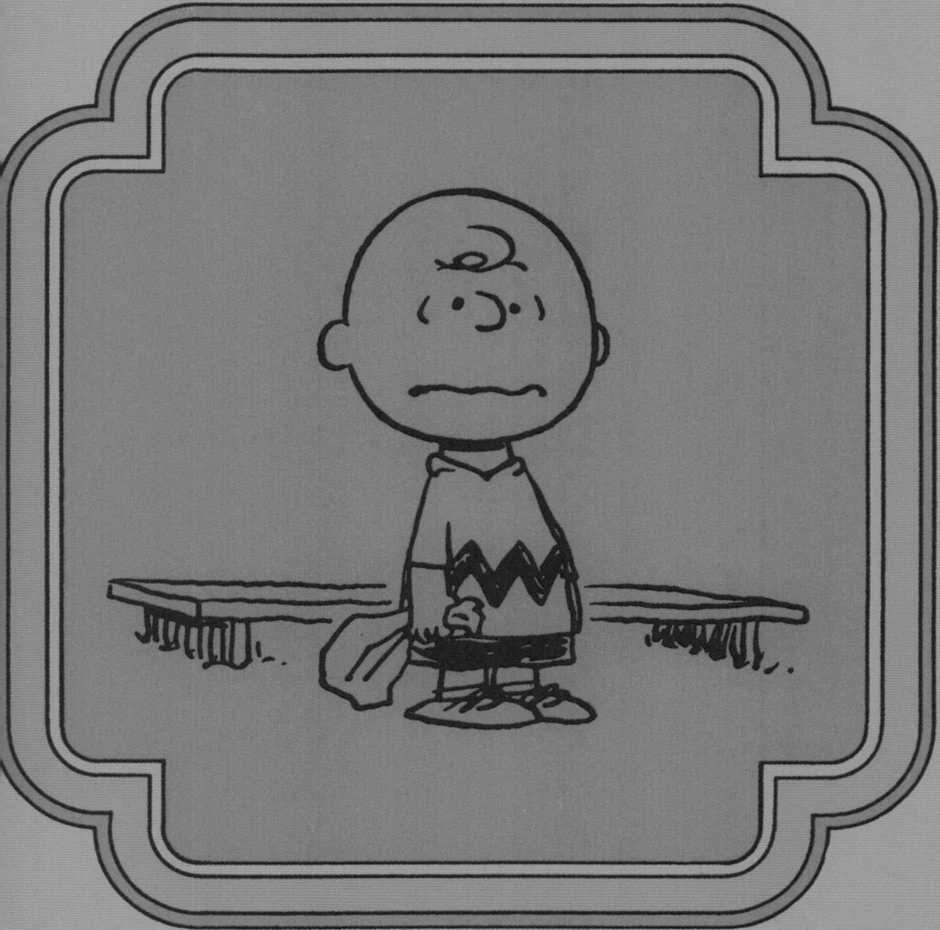

Love is
being happy
just knowing
that she's
happy…but
that isn't so easy

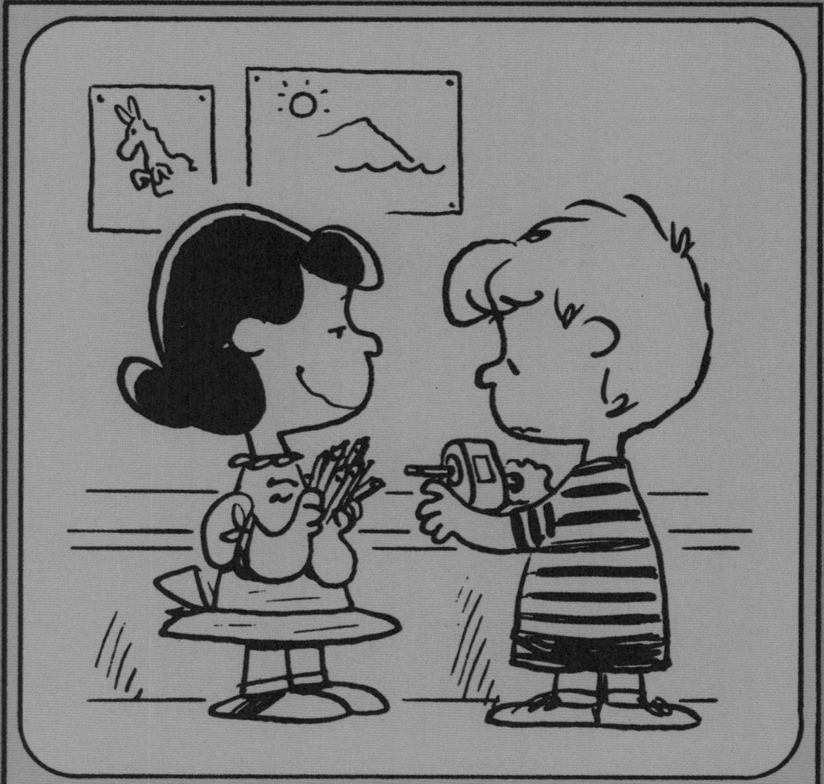

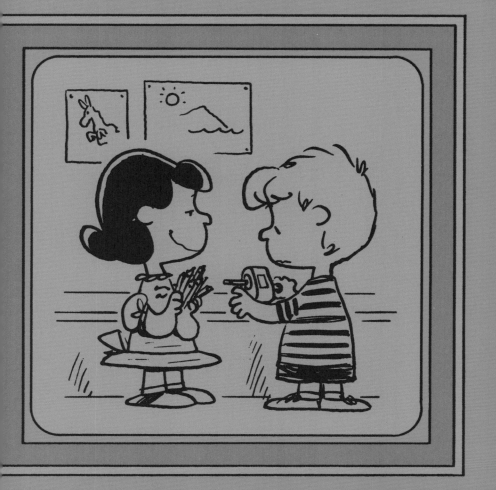

Love is
meeting
someone
by the pencil
sharpener

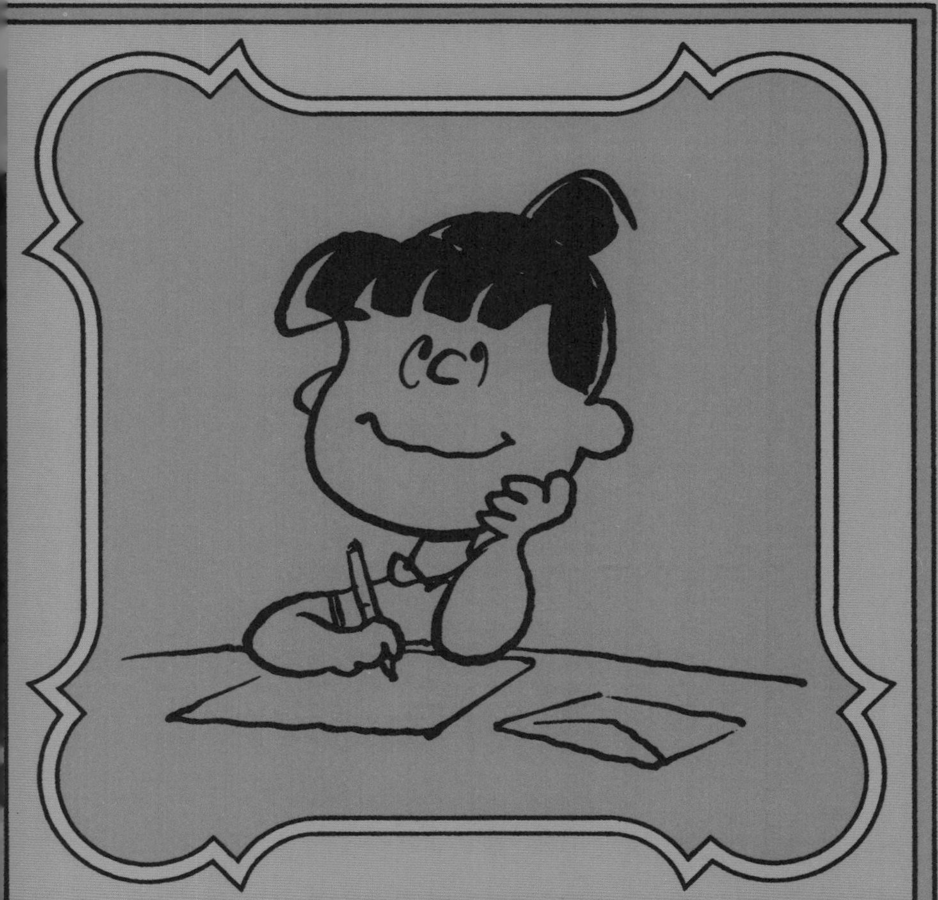

Love is
committing
yourself
in writing

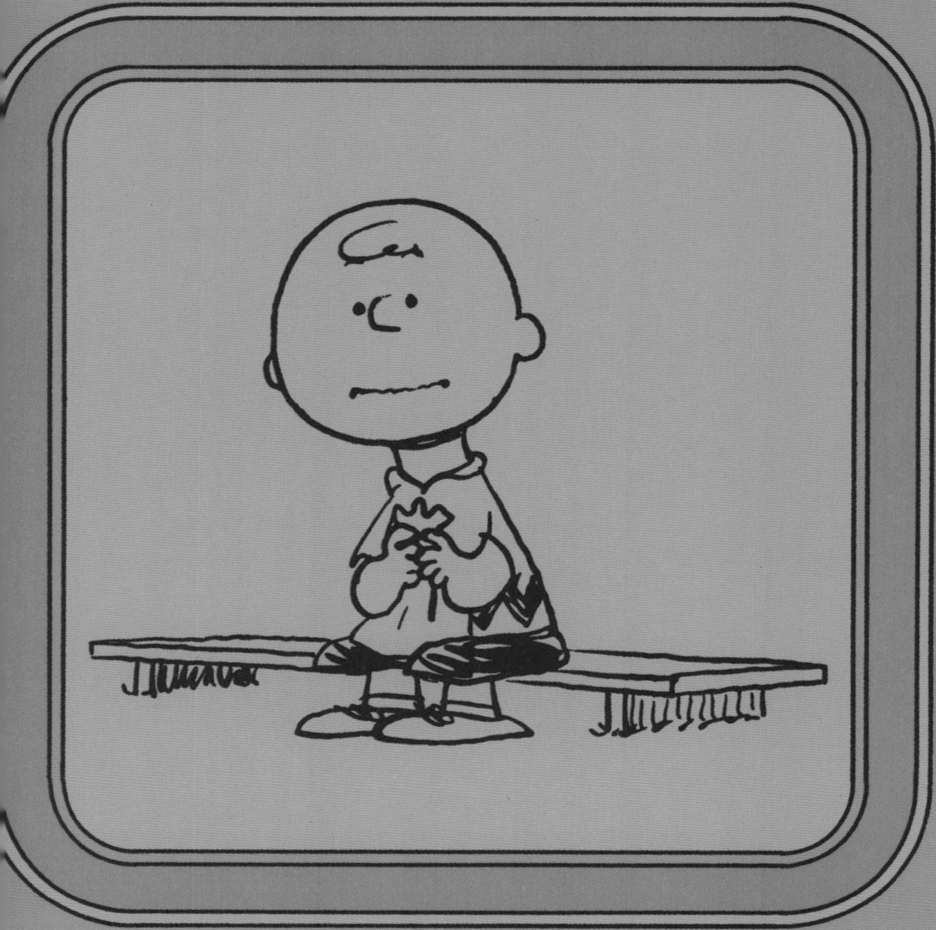

Love is
being able to spot
her clear across
the playground
among
four hundred
other kids

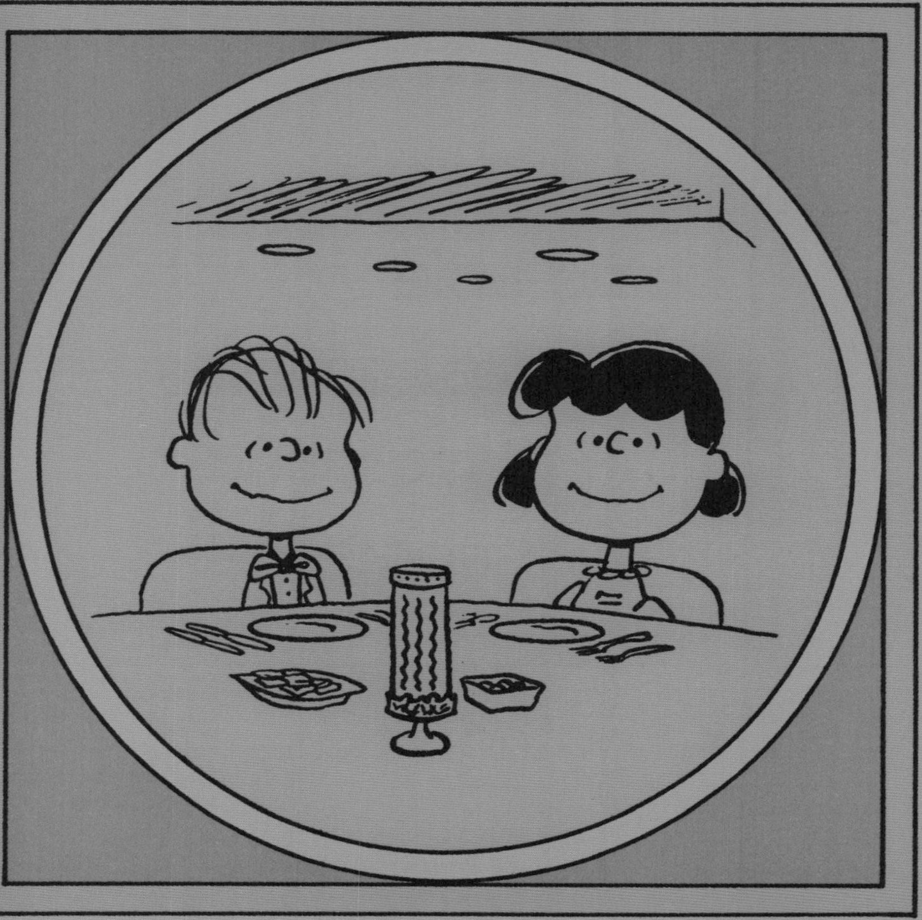

Love is
eating out
with your
whole family

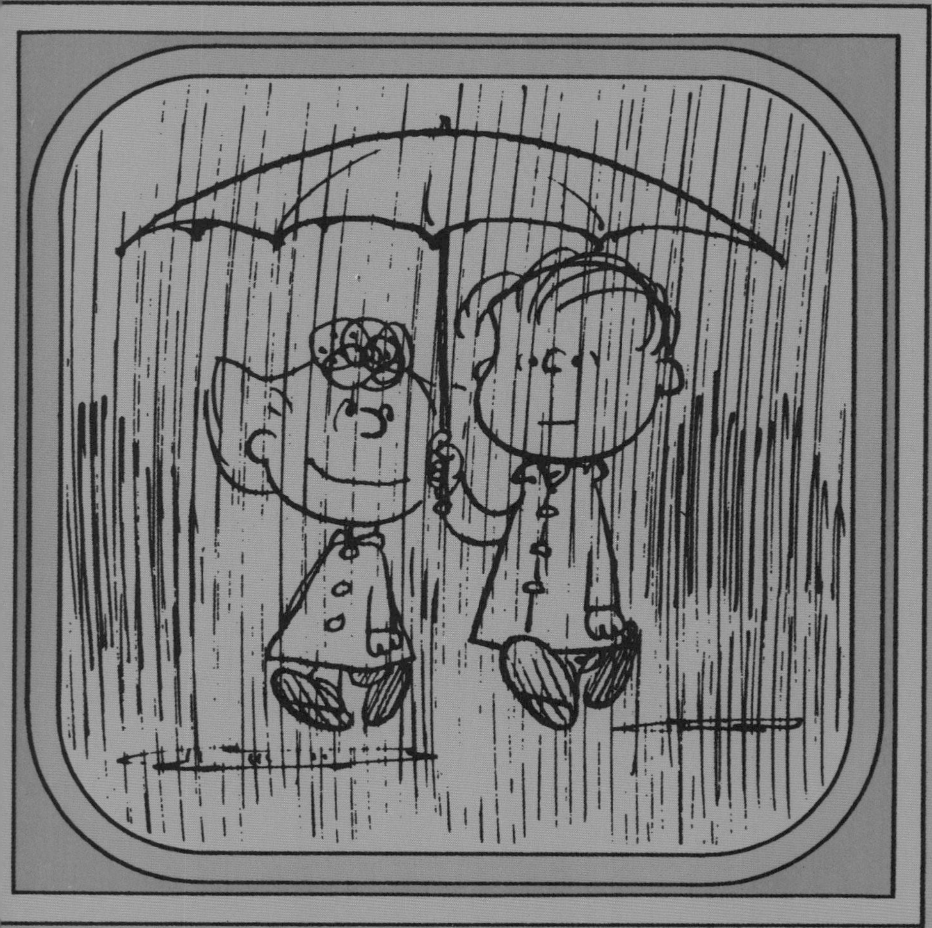

Love is
walking
in the rain
together

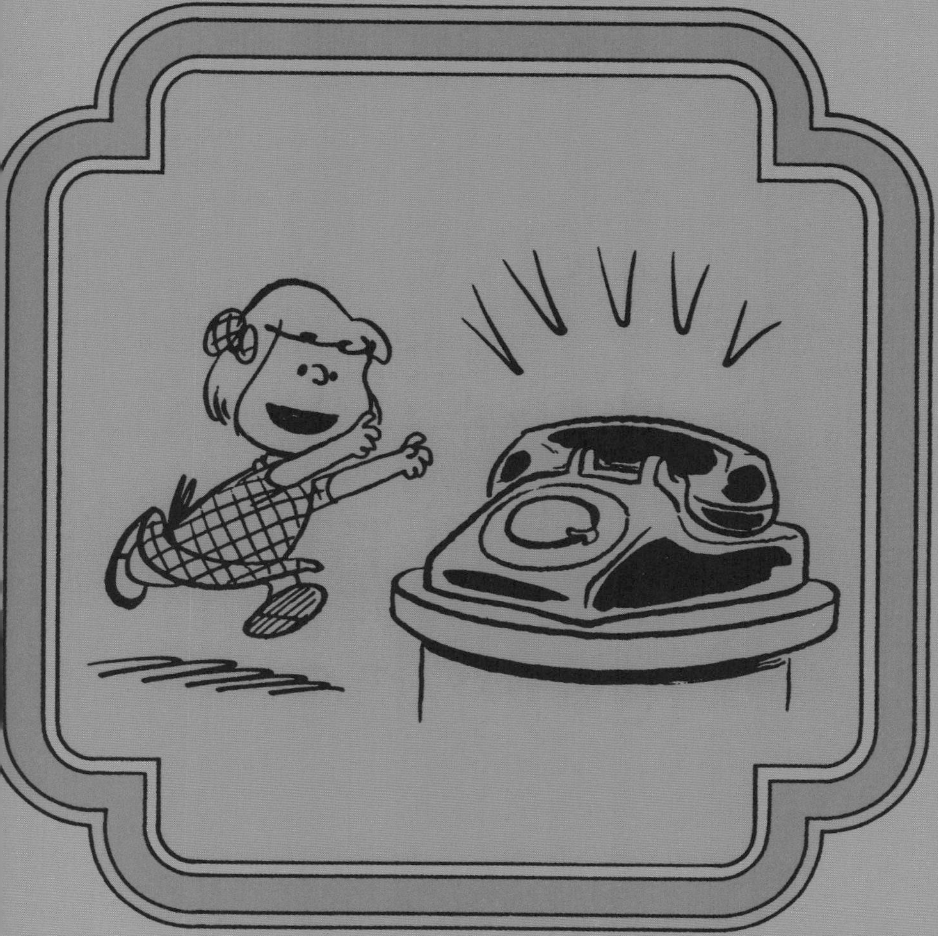

Love is

a

phone

call

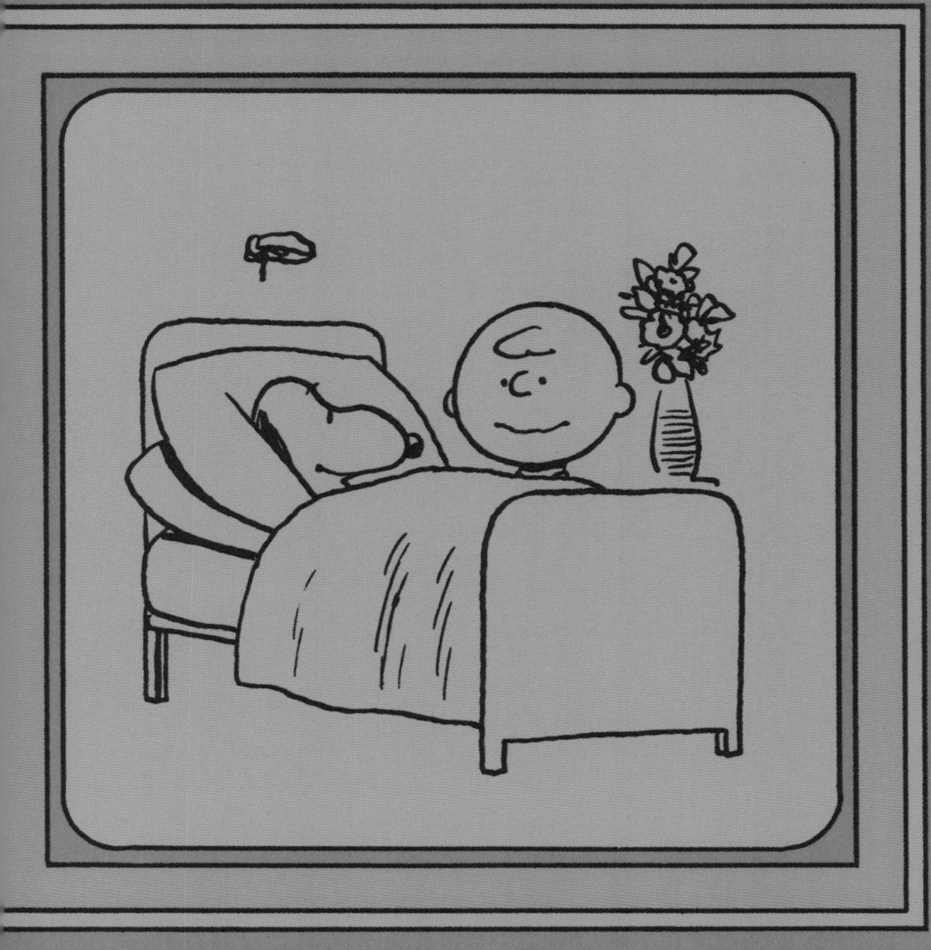

Love is
visiting
a sick
friend

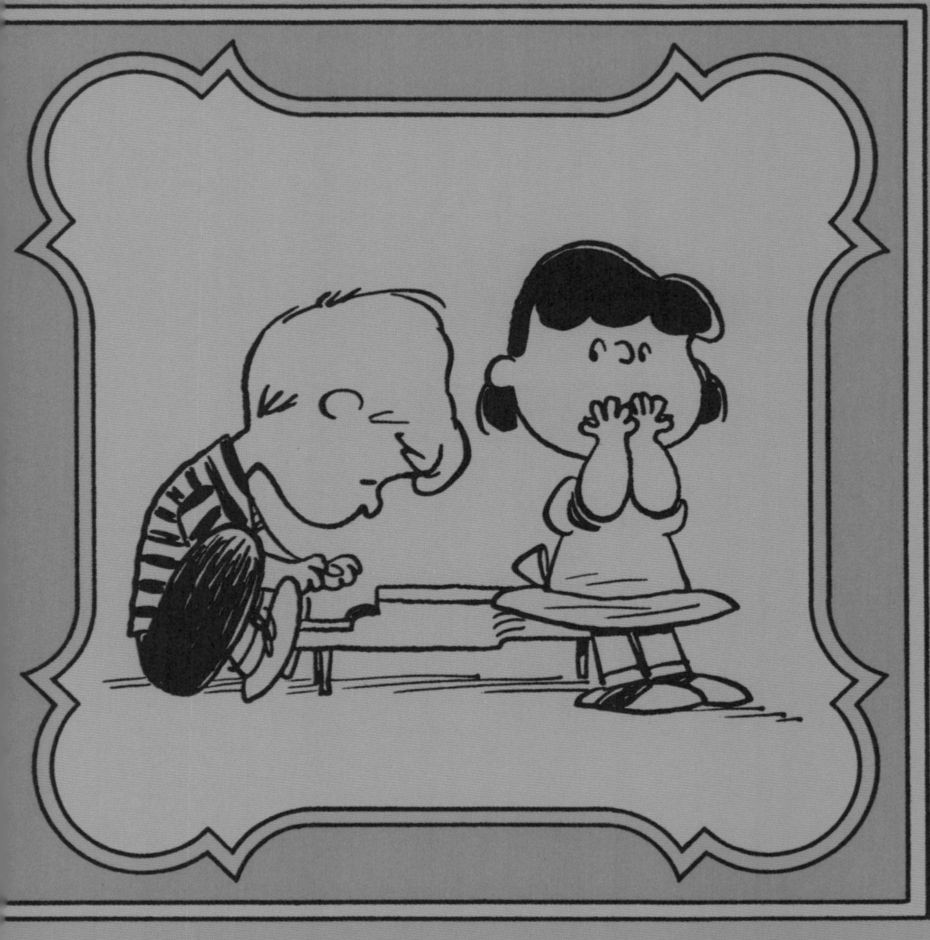

Love is not nagging

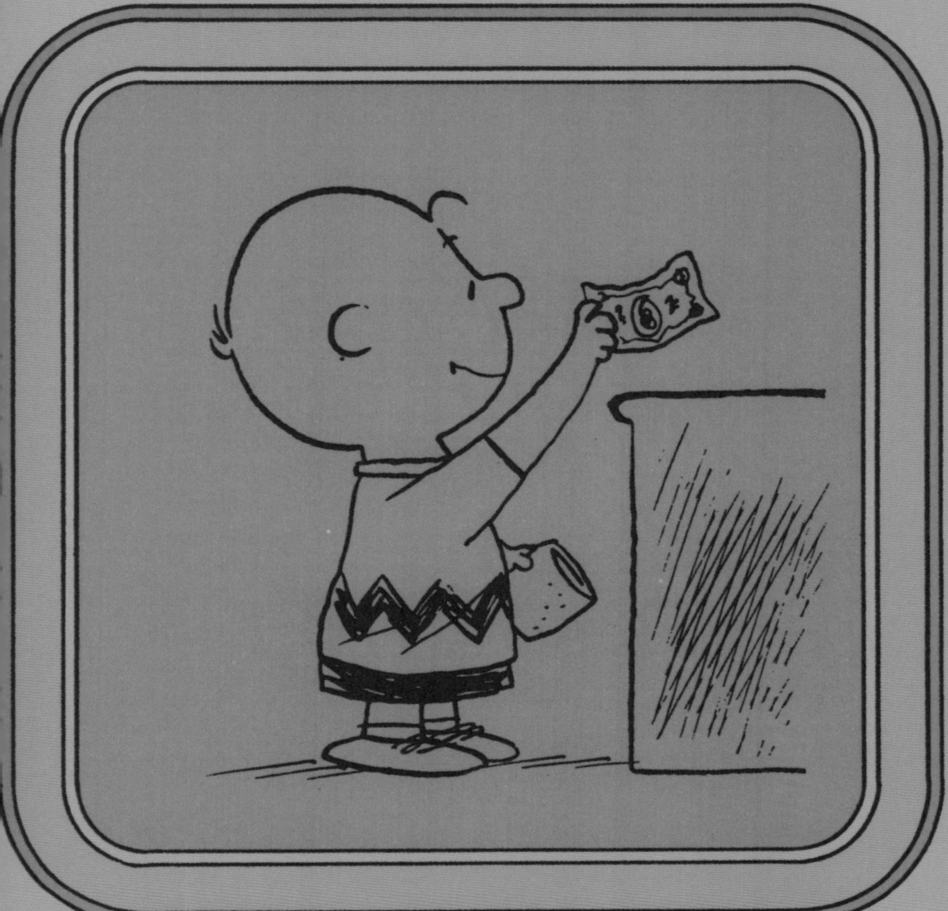

Love is
buying
somebody
a present
with your
own money

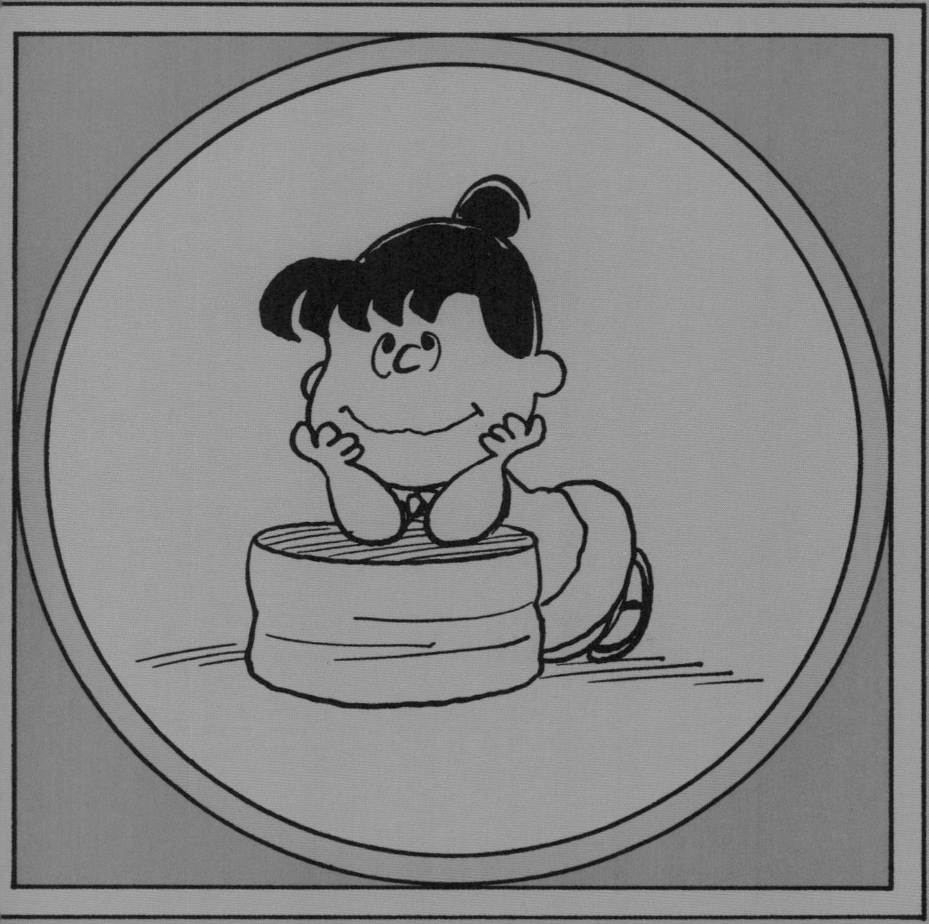

Love is
wondering
what he's doing
right now this
very moment

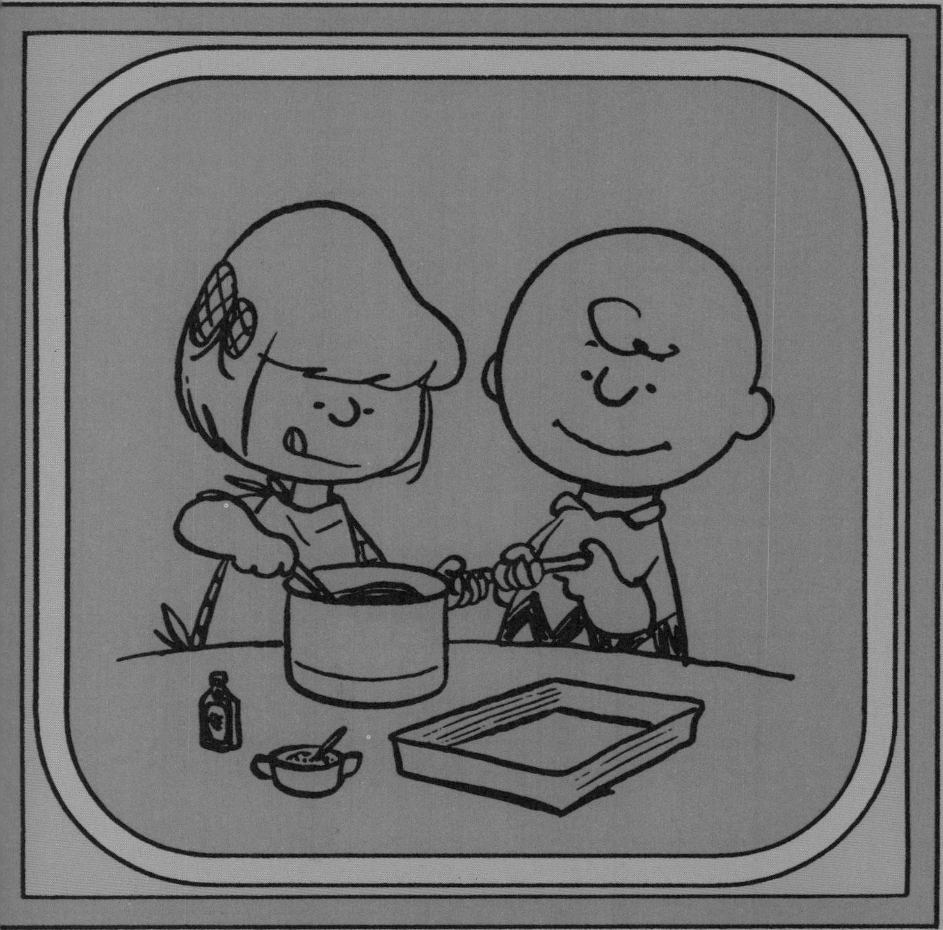

Love is
making
fudge
together

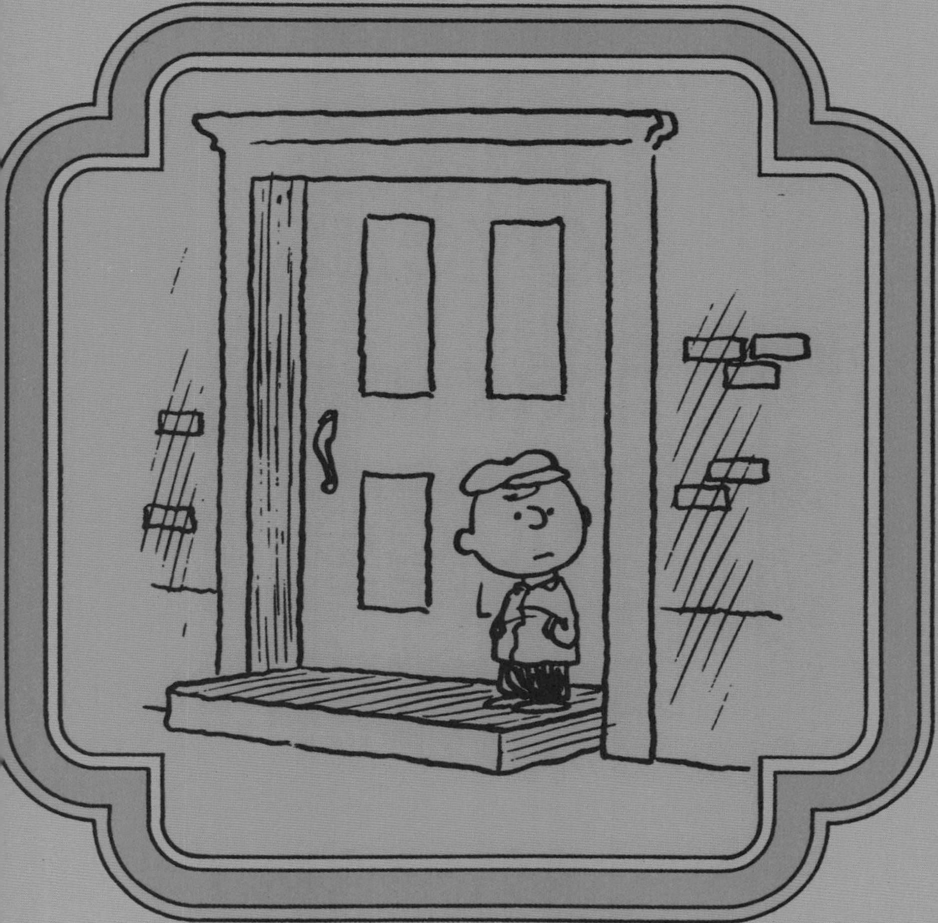

Love is
standing in
a doorway just
to see her
if she comes
walking by

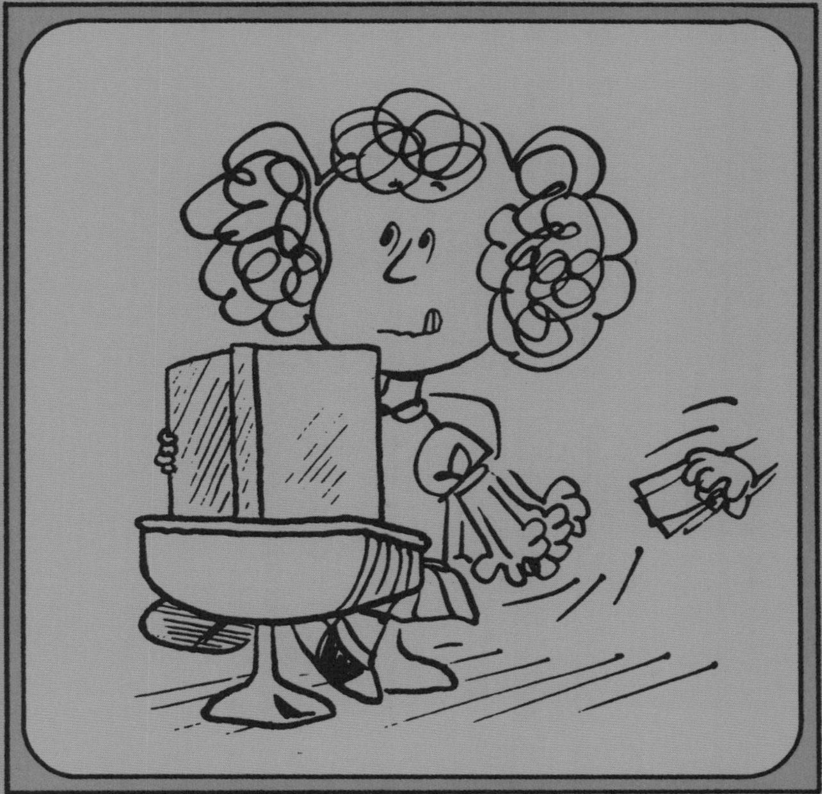

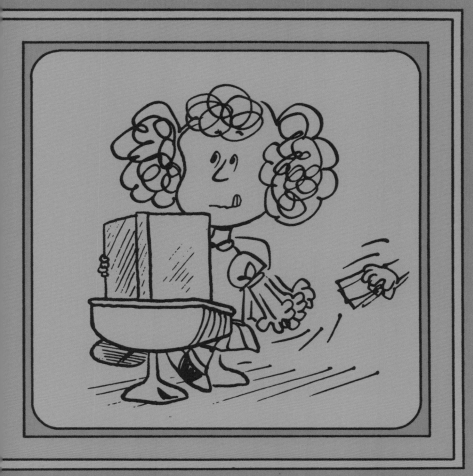

Love is passing notes back and forth in school

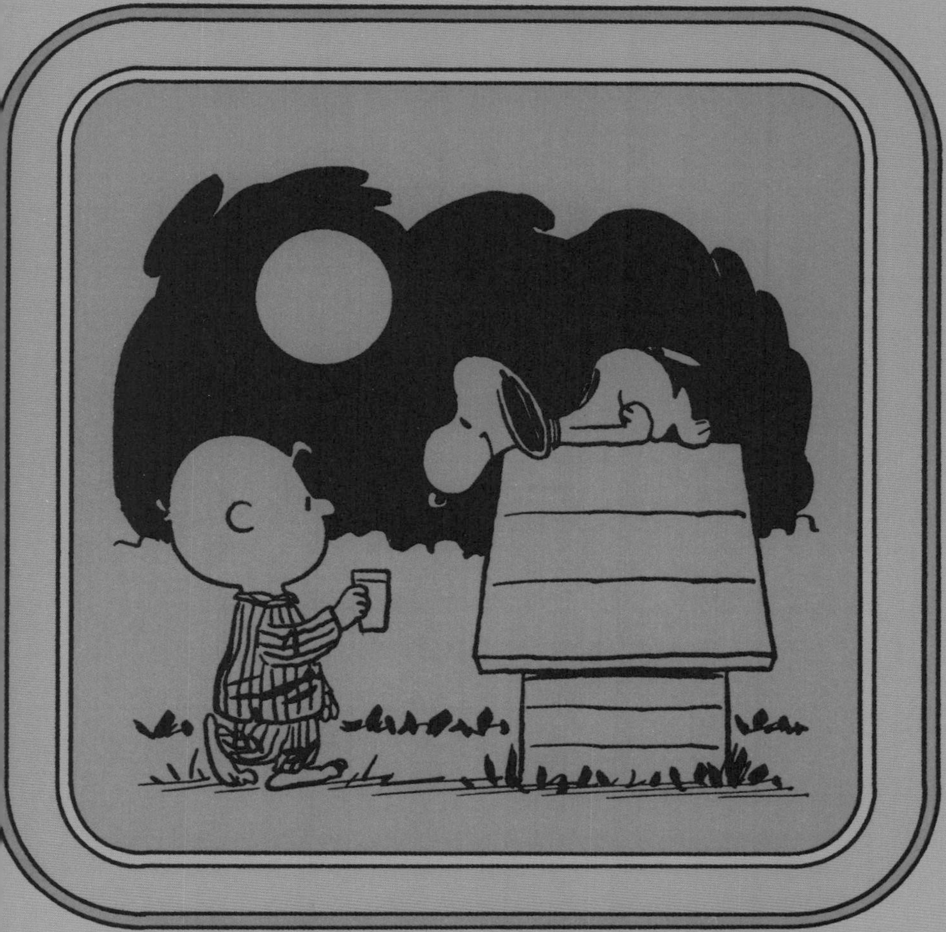

Love is
getting someone
a glass of water
in the middle
of the night

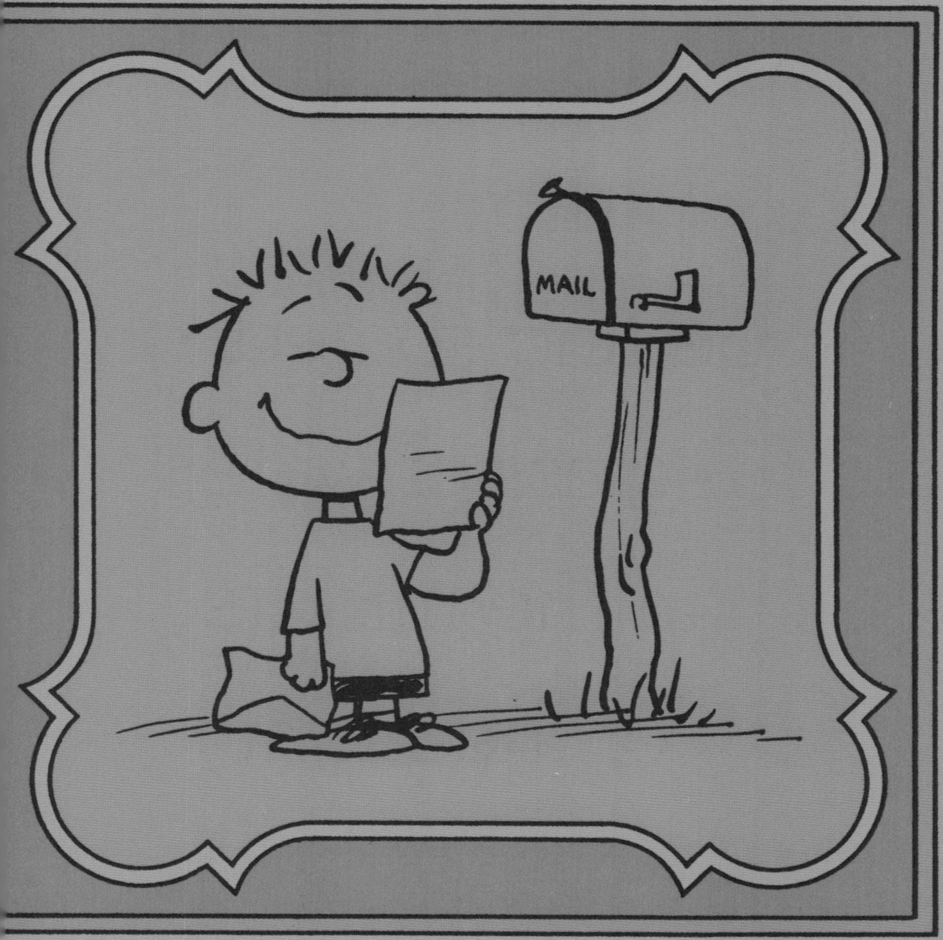
MAIL

Love is
a letter
on pink
stationery

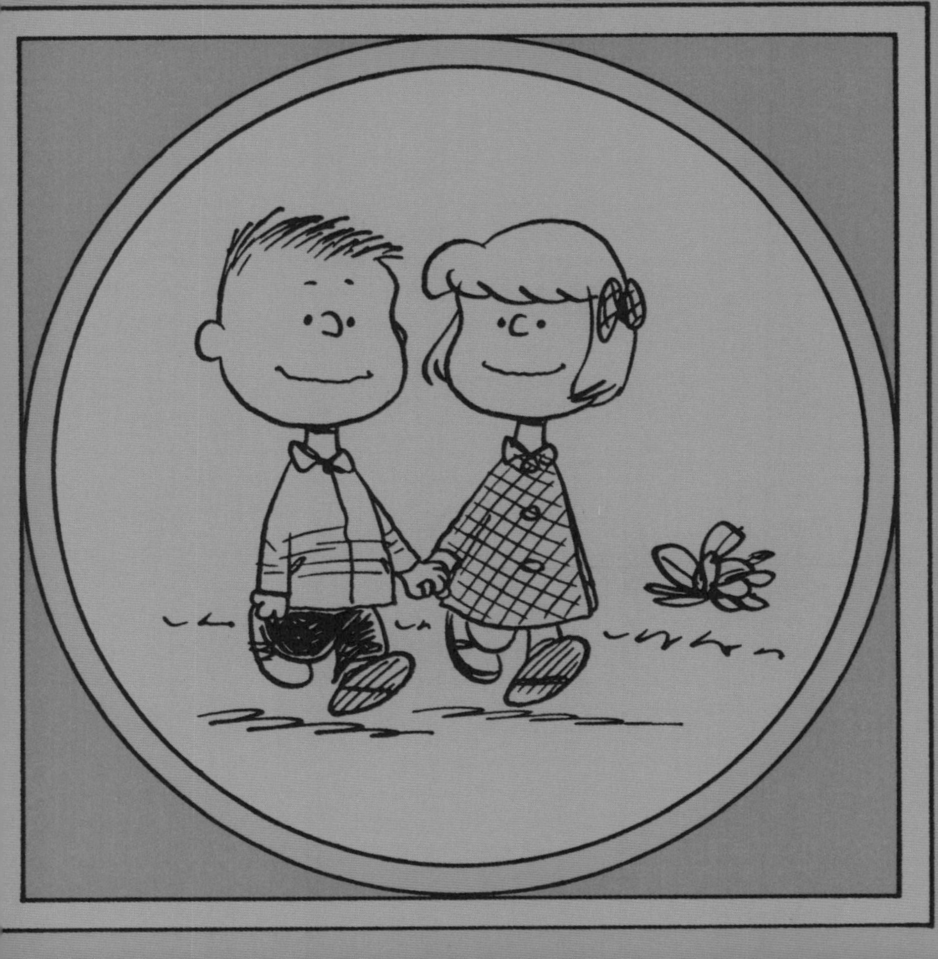

Love is
walking
hand
in hand

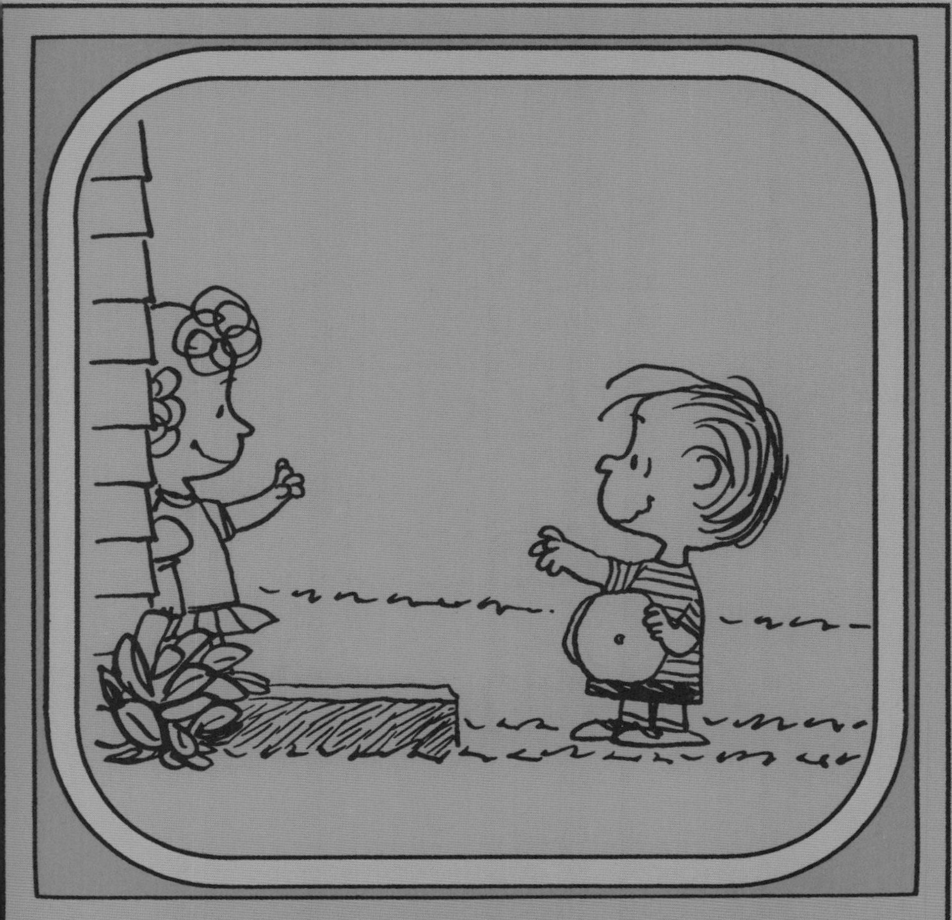

Love is
hating
to say
good-bye

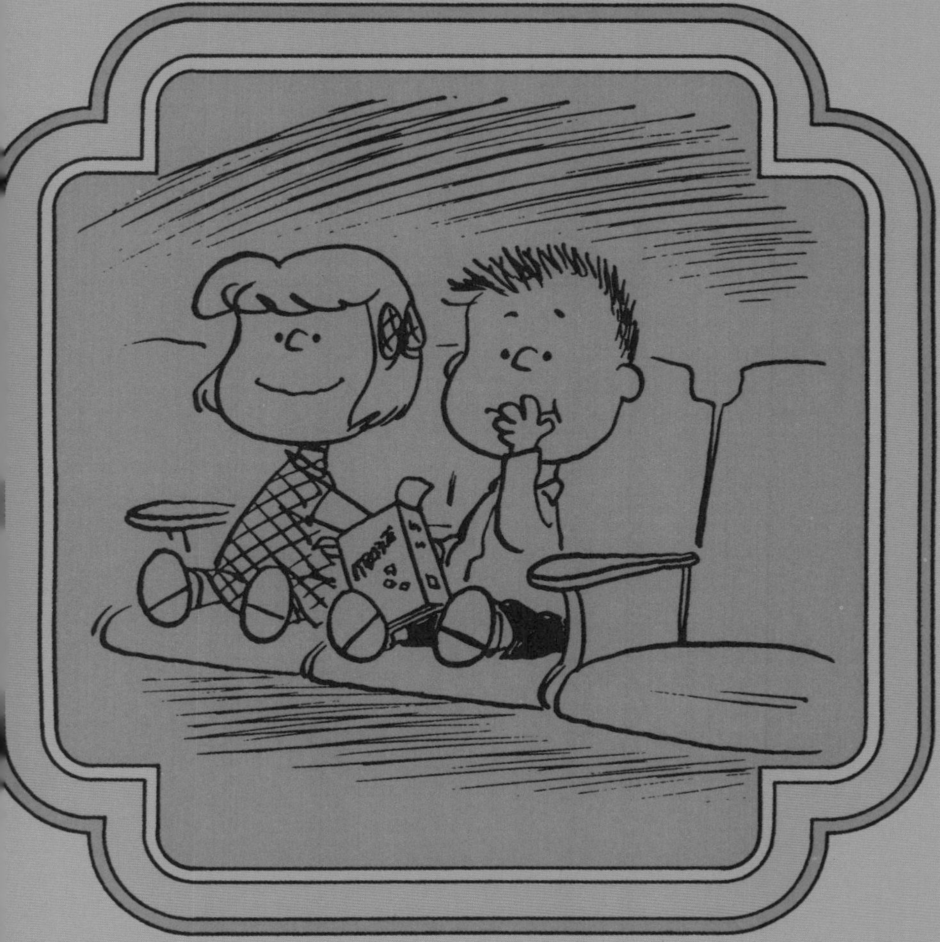

Love is
sharing
your
popcorn

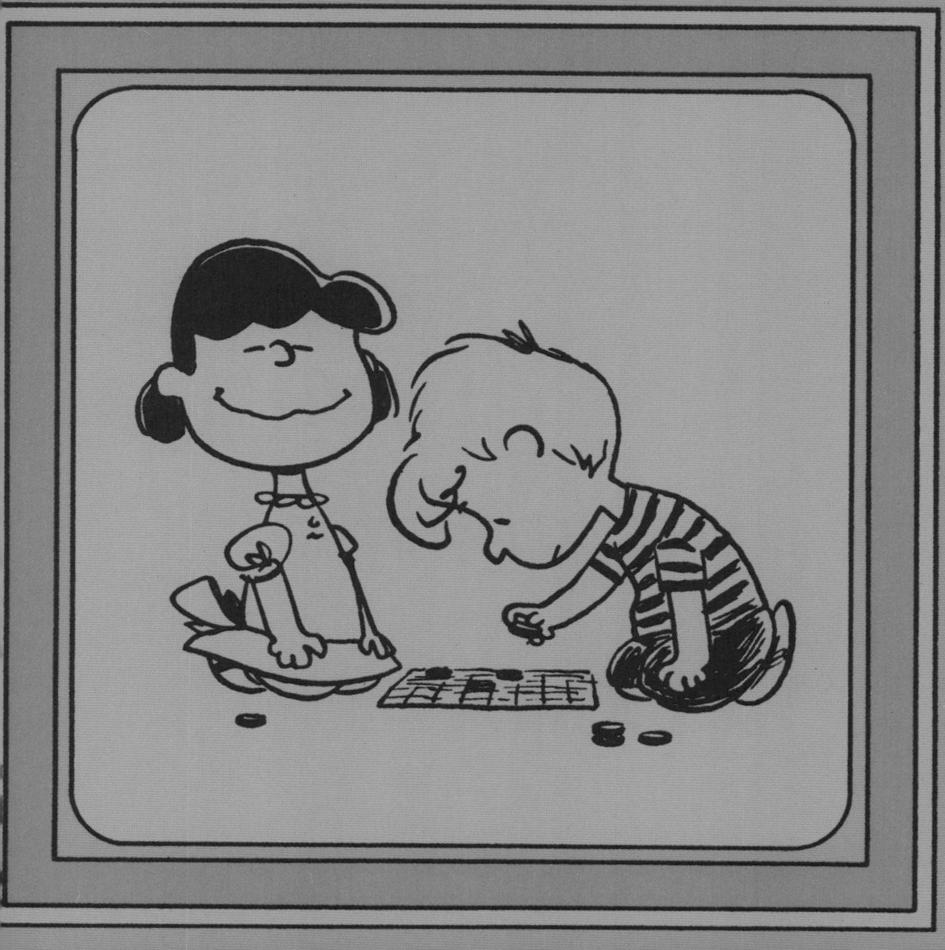

Love is
letting him win
even though you
know you could
slaughter him

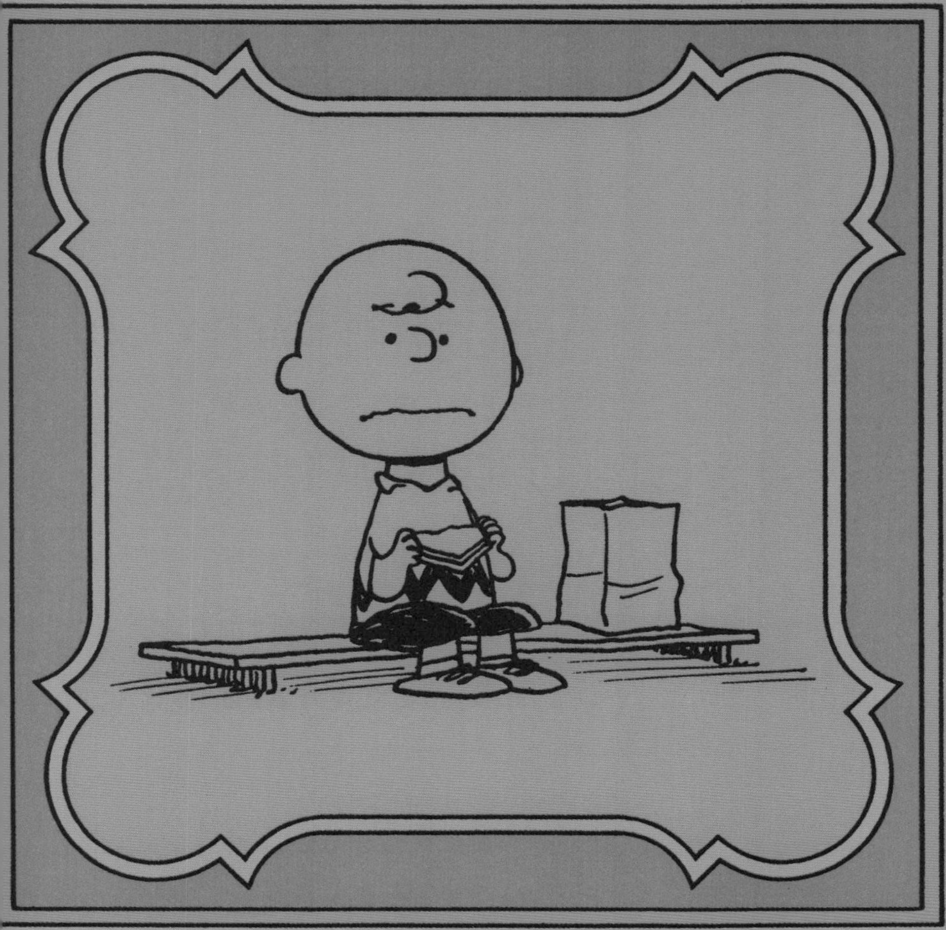

Love is
wishing you had
nerve enough to
go over and
talk with that little girl
with the red hair

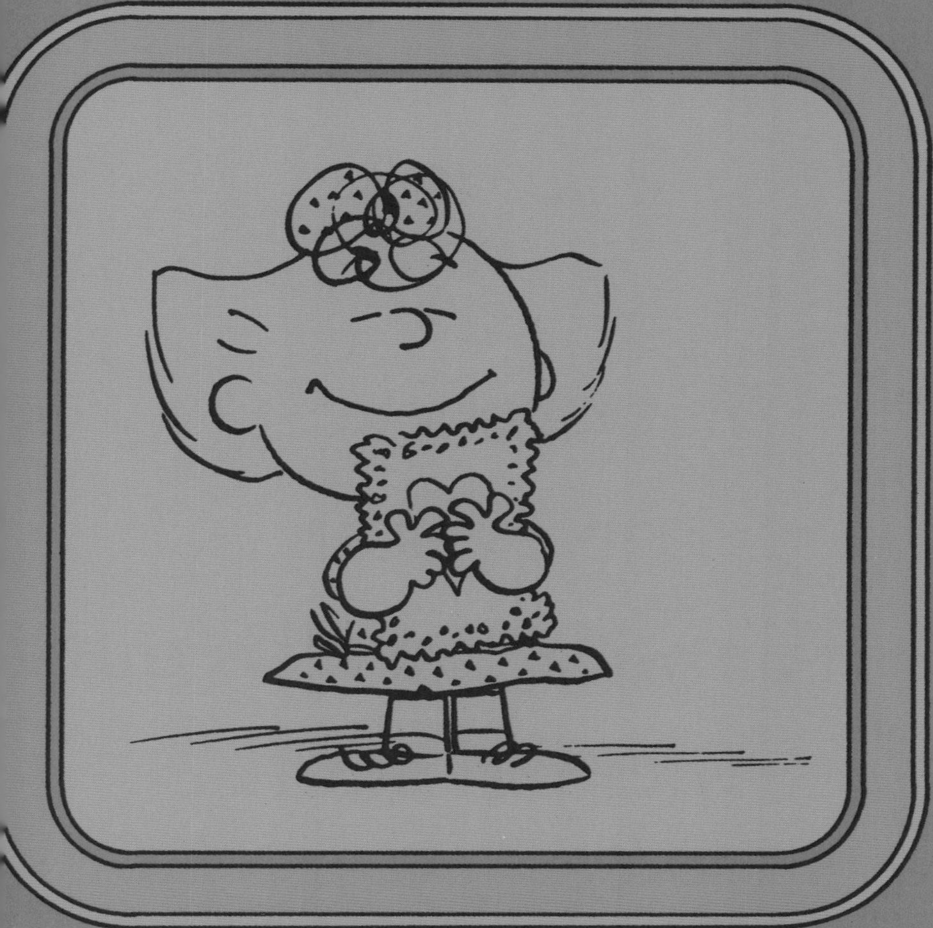

Love is
a valentine
with lace
all around
the edges

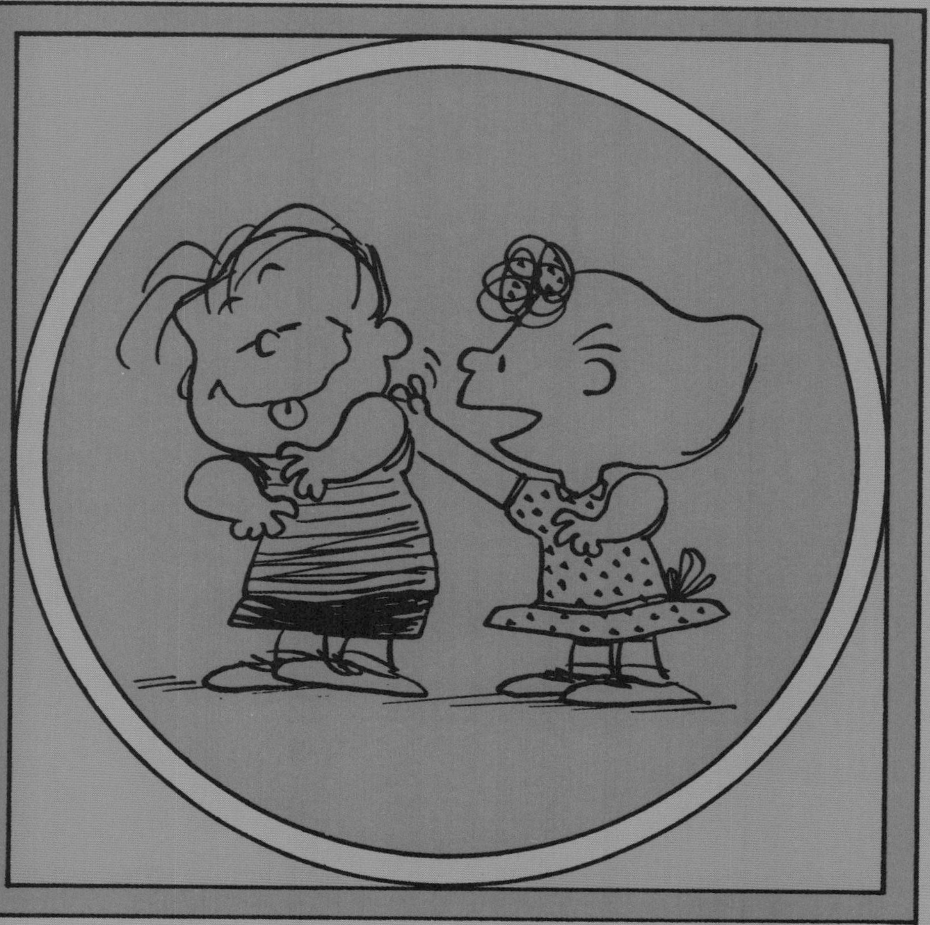

Love
is
tickling

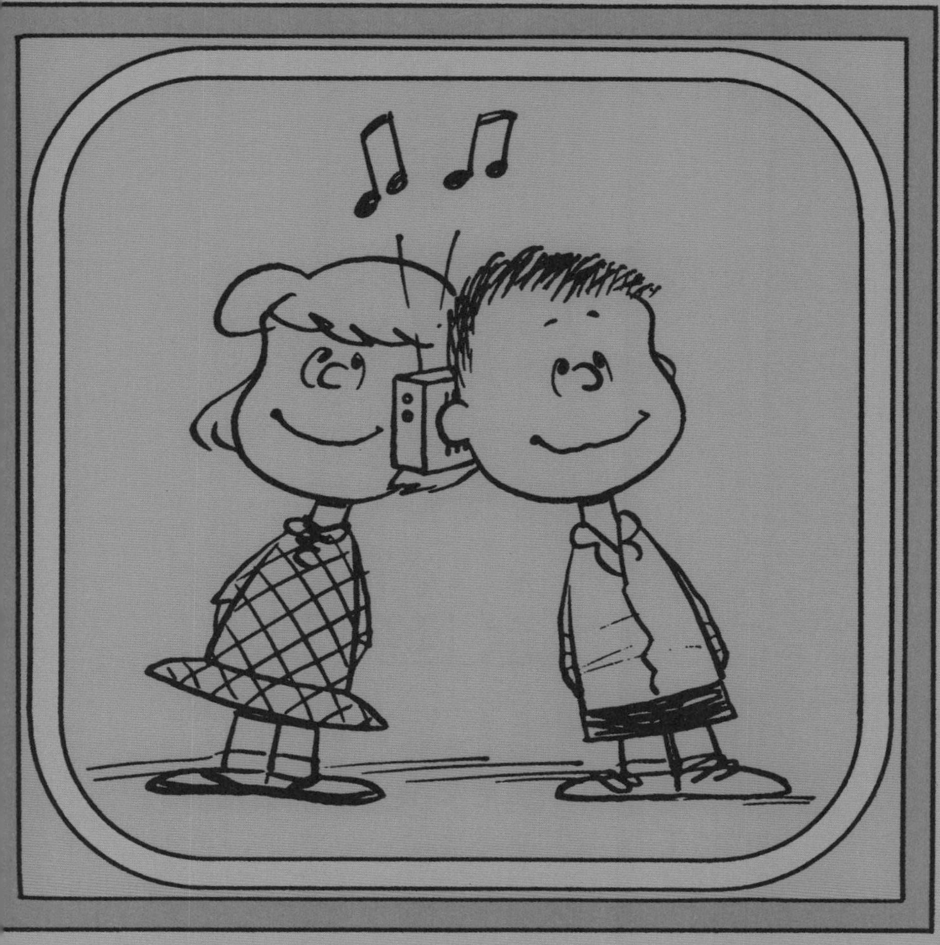

Love
is
having
a
special song

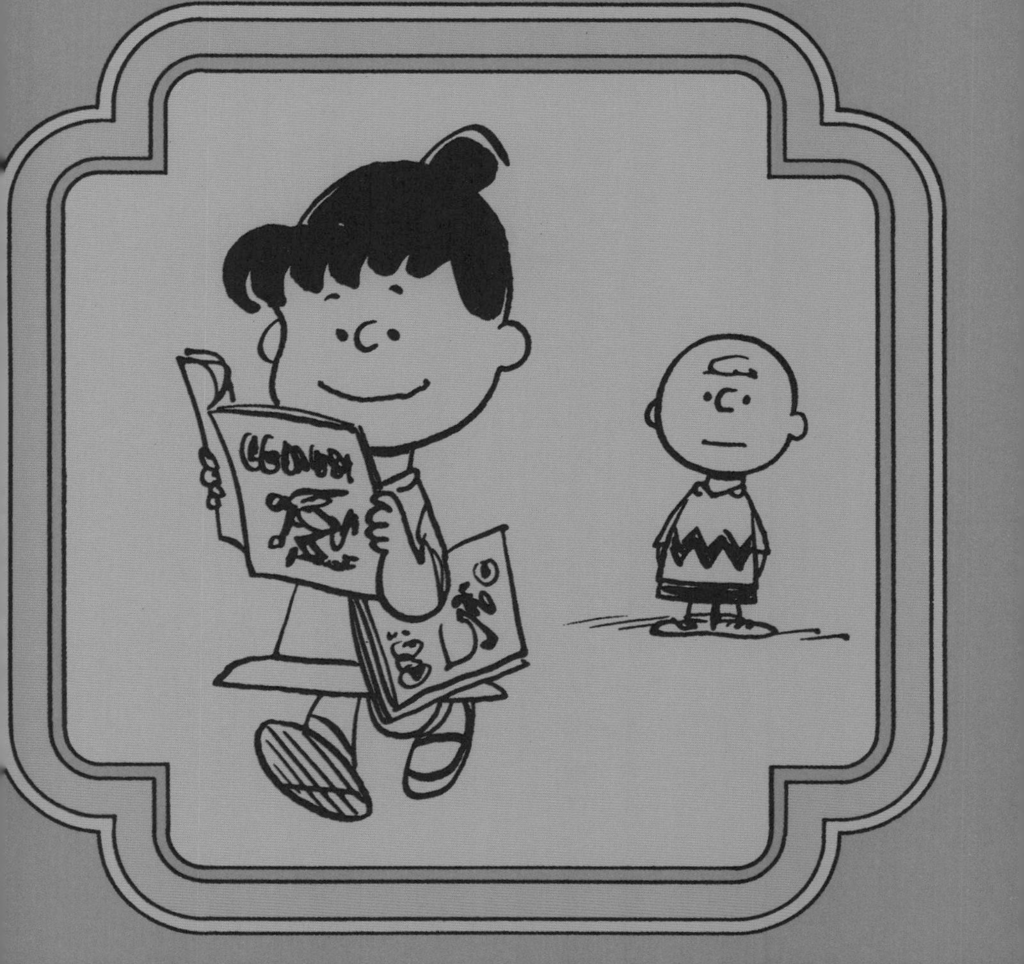

Love is
loaning your
best comic
magazines

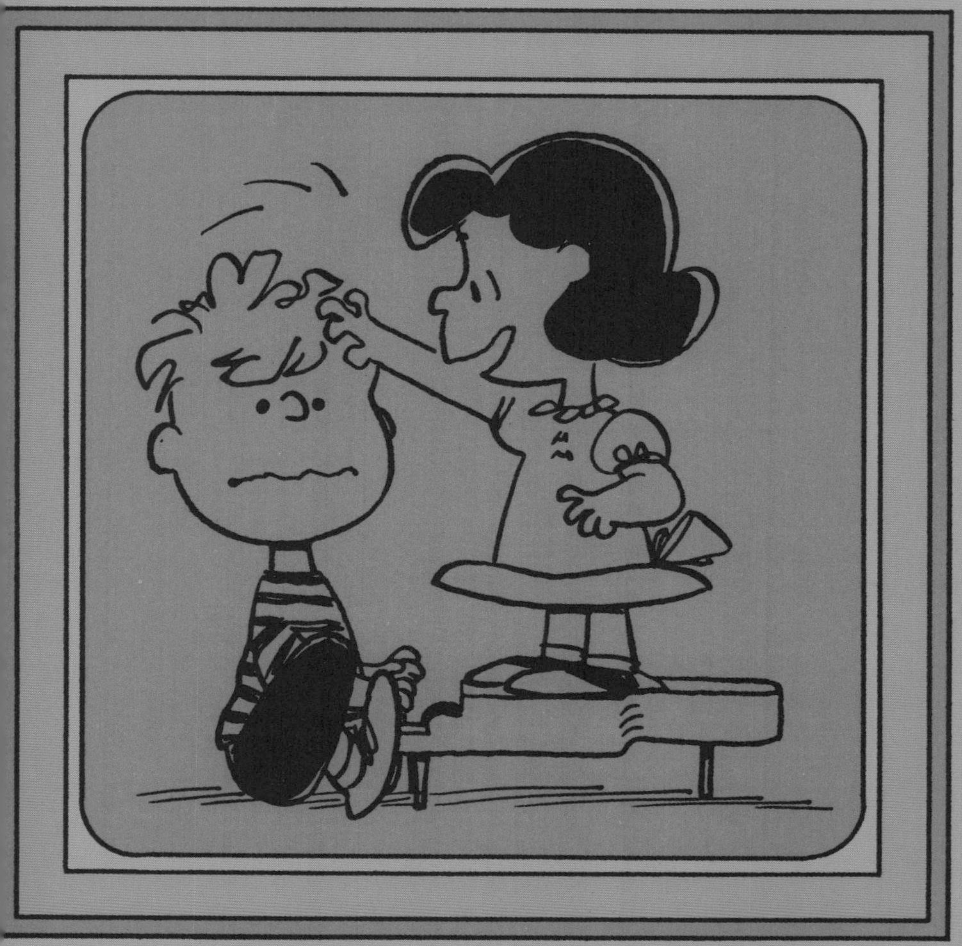

Love is
mussing up
someone's
hair

LOVE
IS WALKING
HAND IN HAND

PENGUIN WORKSHOP
An Imprint of Penguin Random House LLC

© 1965 Peanuts Worldwide LLC. All rights reserved. This edition published in 2018 by Penguin Workshop,
an imprint of Penguin Random House LLC, 345 Hudson Street, New York, New York 10014.
PENGUIN and PENGUIN WORKSHOP are trademarks of Penguin Books Ltd, and the
W colophon is a trademark of Penguin Random House LLC. Manufactured in China.

Library of Congress Cataloging-in-Publication Data is available.

ISBN 9781524789947   10 9 8 7 6 5 4

LOVE

IS WALKING

HAND IN HAND

BY

CHARLES M.

SCHULZ

TO:

_____

FROM:

_____

"(Well, what do you know?)"

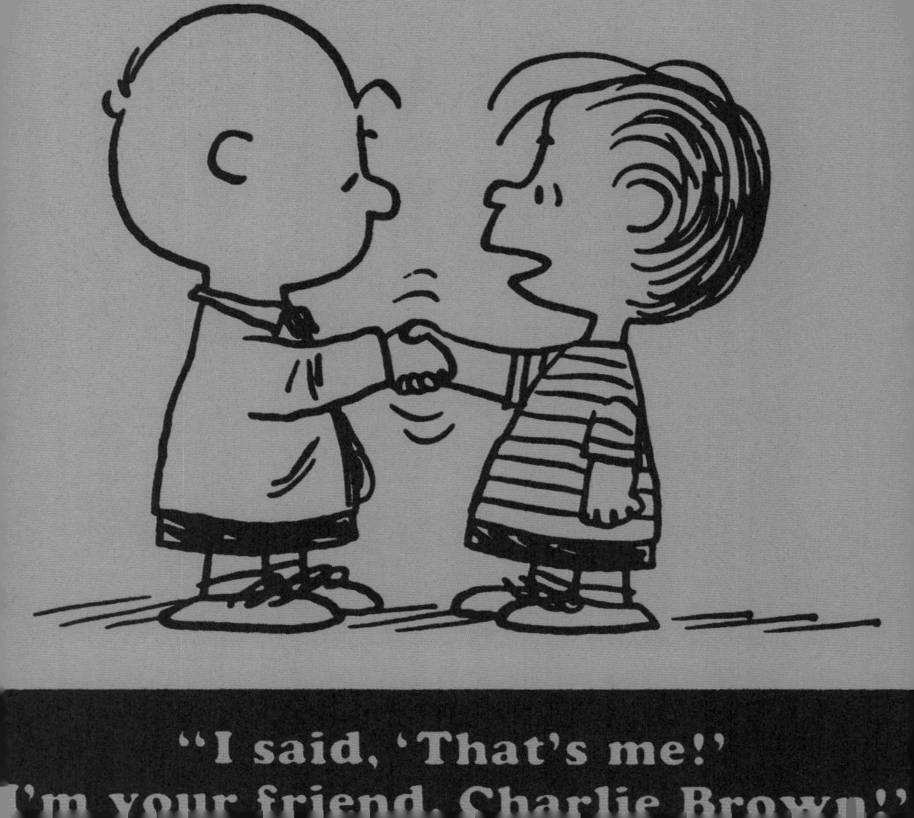

"I said, 'That's me!'
I'm your friend, Charlie Brown!'

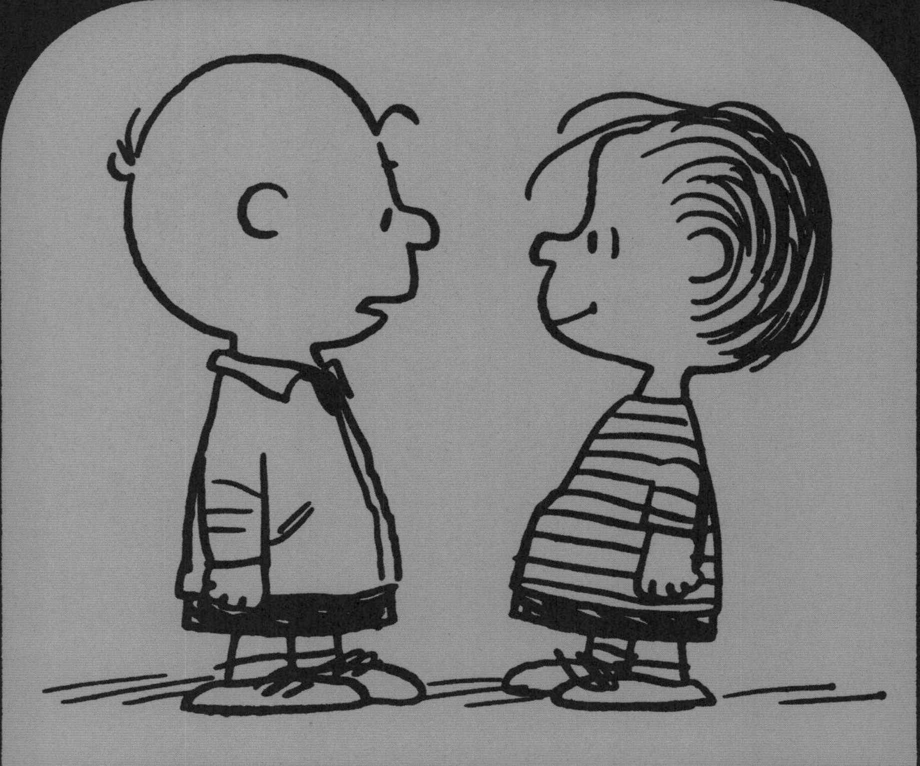

"What?"

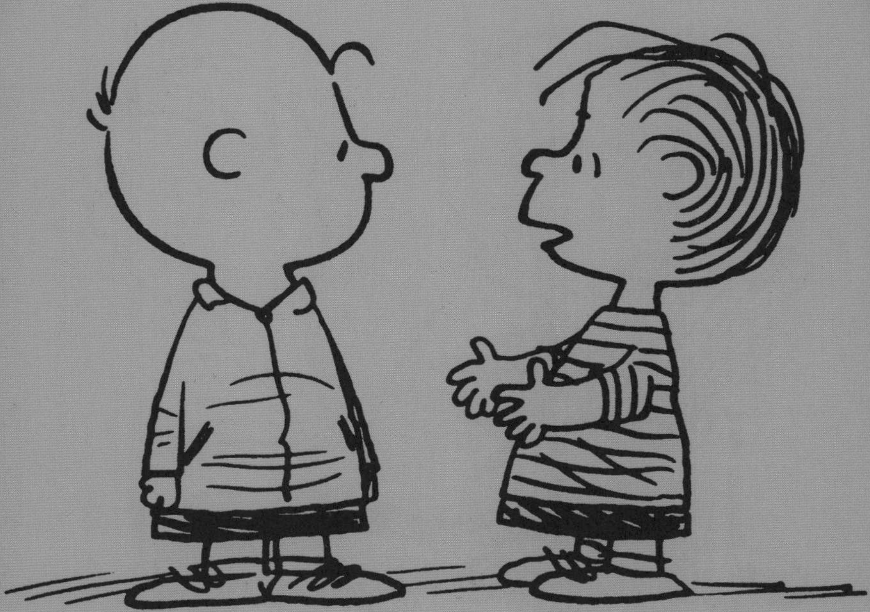

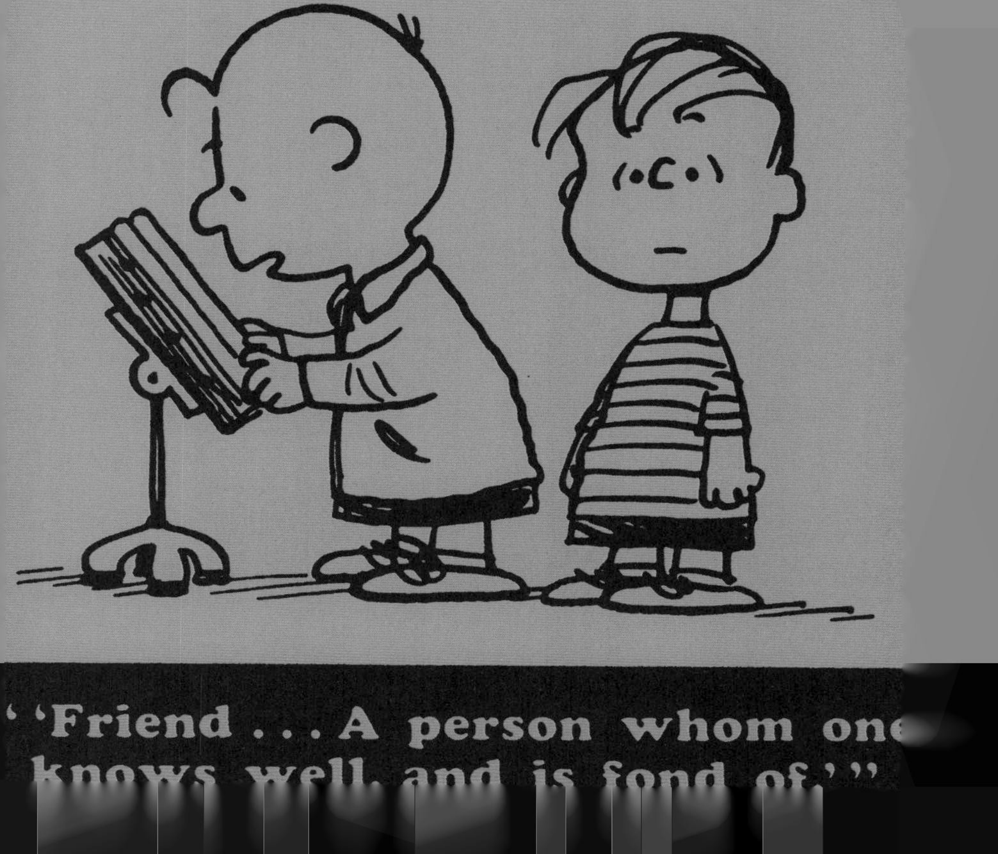

''Friend . . . A person whom one knows well, and is fond of.''

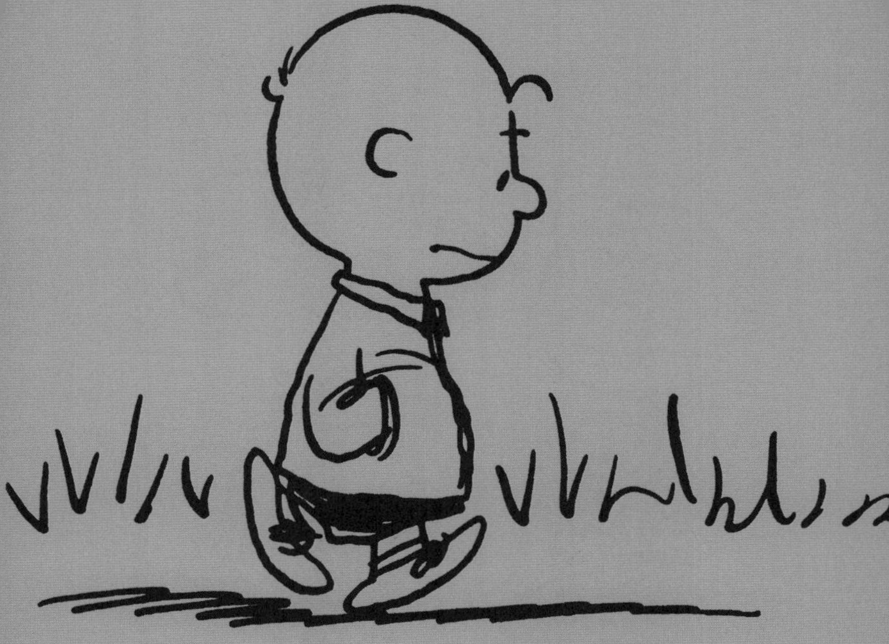

"All these definitions have got me confused."

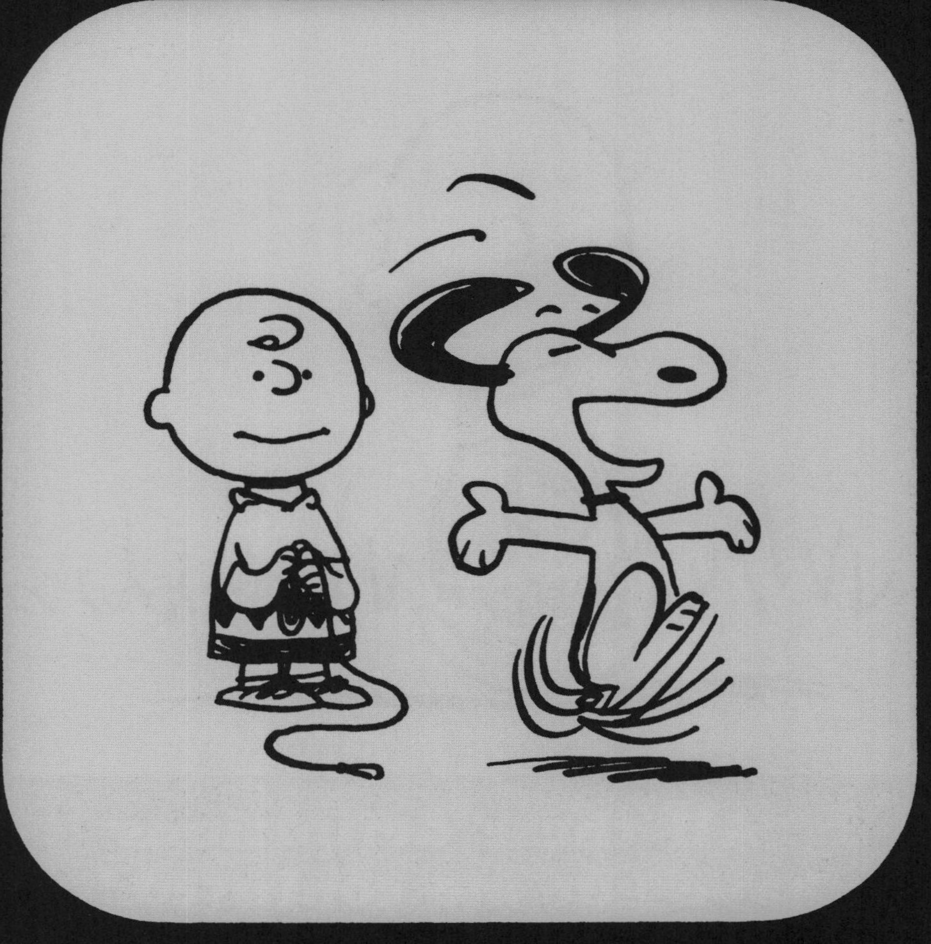

"A friend is someone who takes off the leash!"

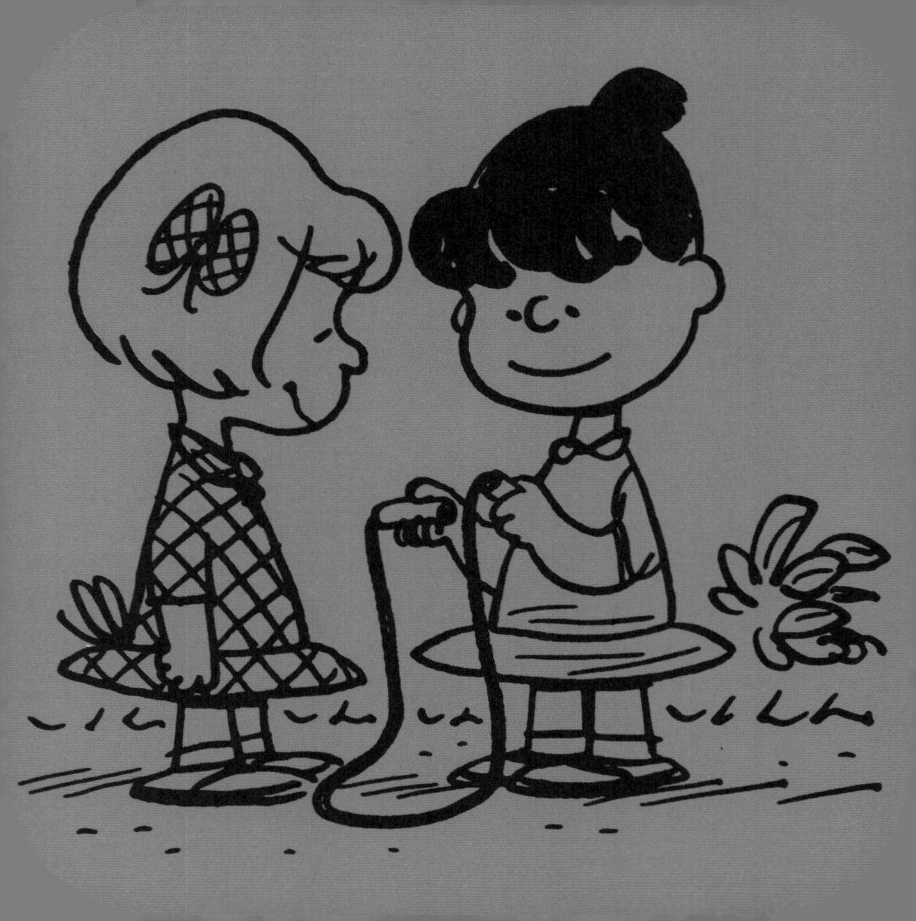

"A friend
is someone who
doesn't criticize
something you
just bought."

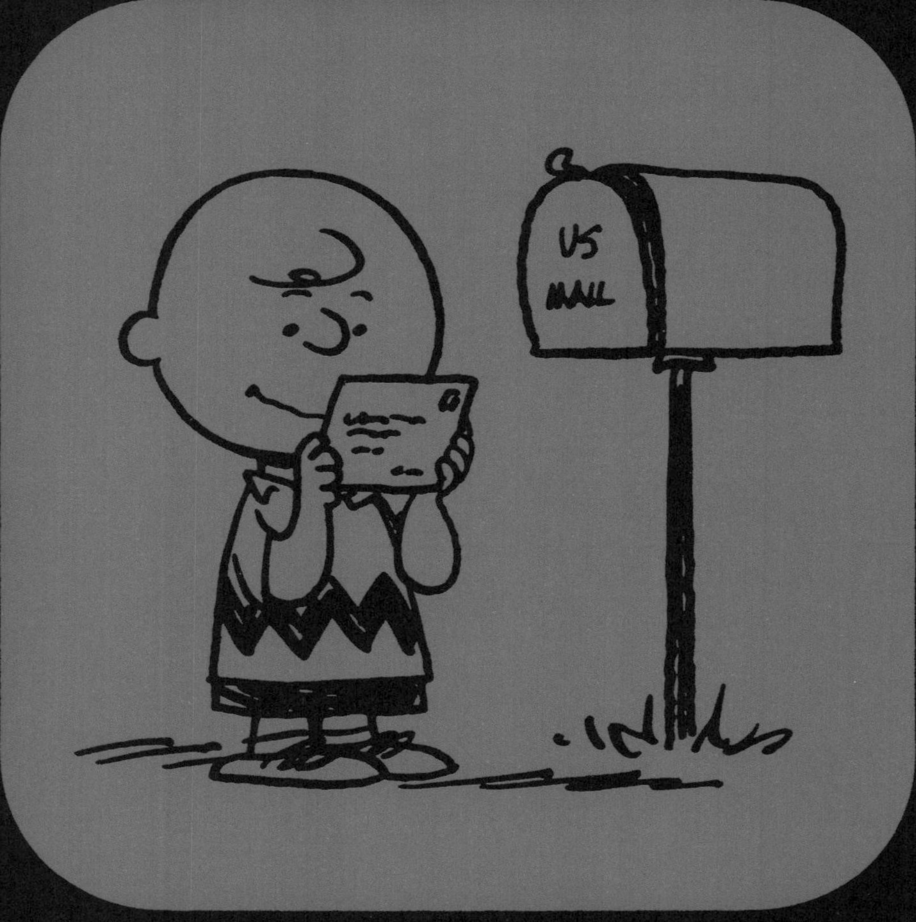
US
MAIL

"A friend is someone who sends you a postcard when he's on vacation."

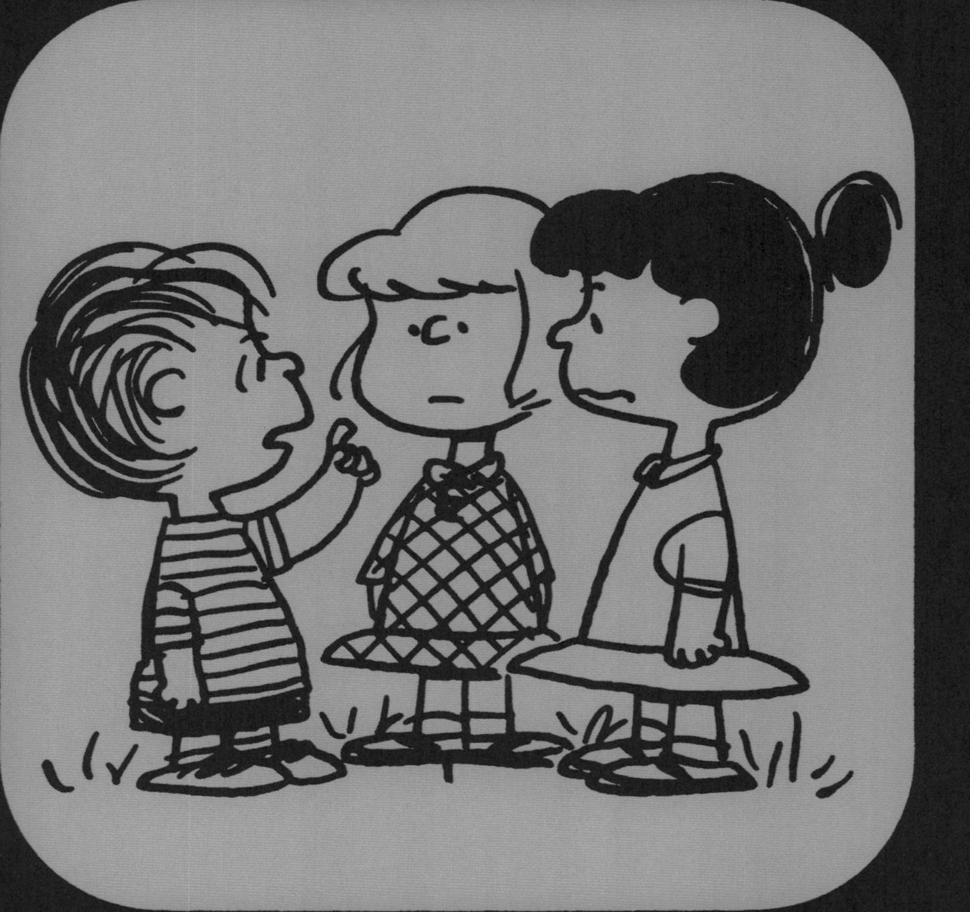

"A friend
is someone who
sticks up for you
when you're
not there."

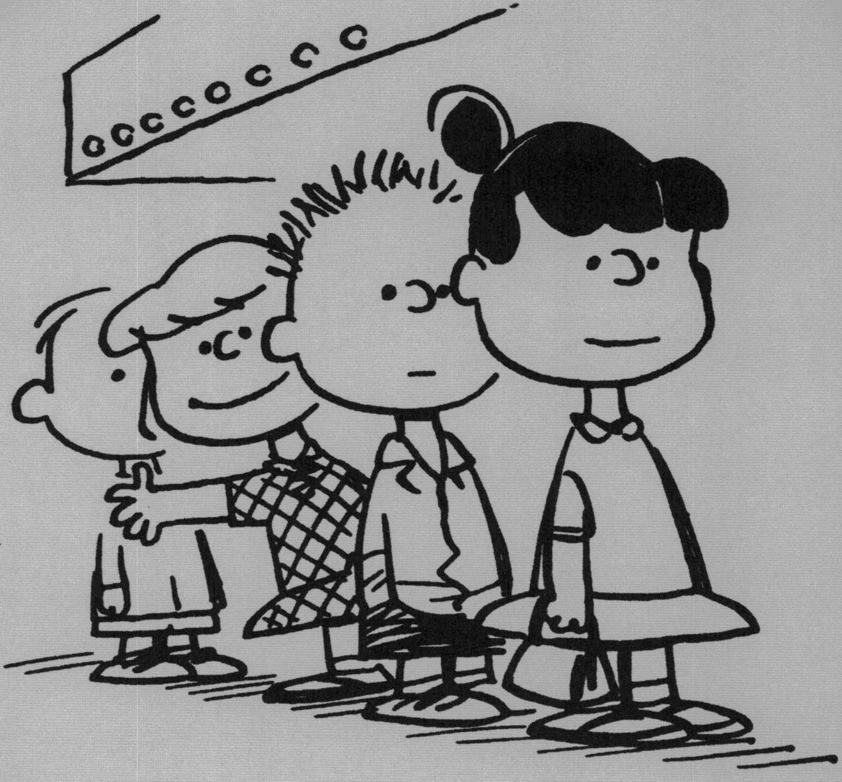

"A friend is someone who will hold a place in line for you."

"A friend
is someone
who can't stand
the same sort of
music you can't
stand!"

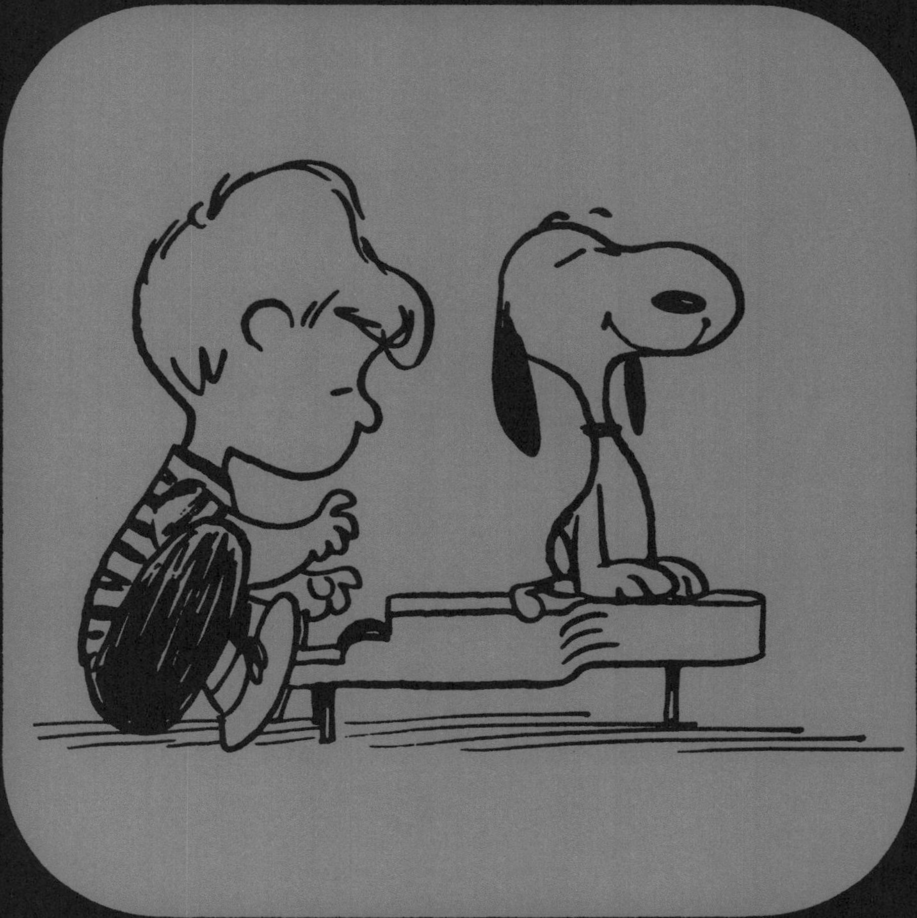

"A friend is someone who likes the same music you like."

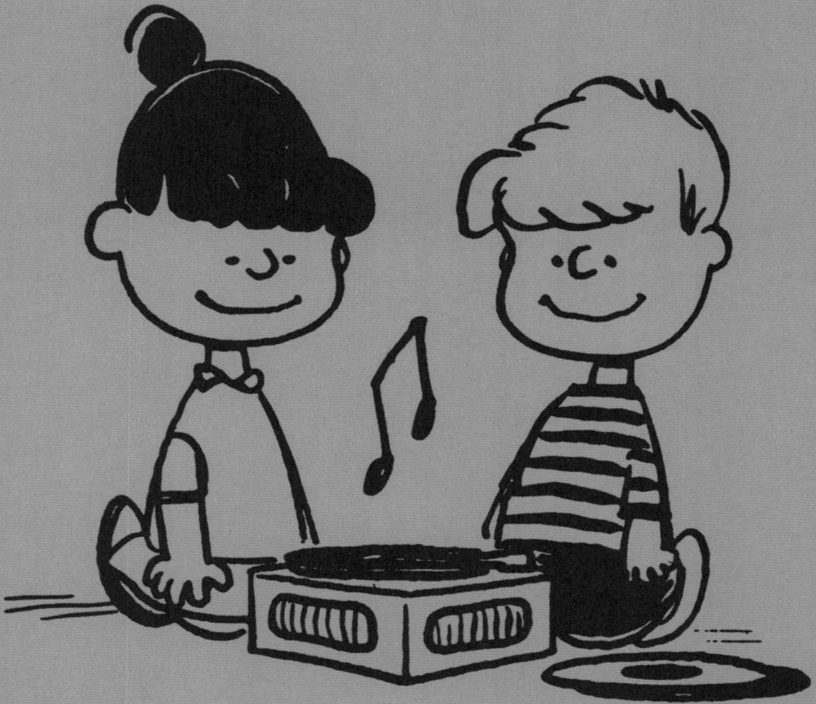

"A friend
is someone
who doesn't think
it's crazy to collect
old Henry Busse
records!"

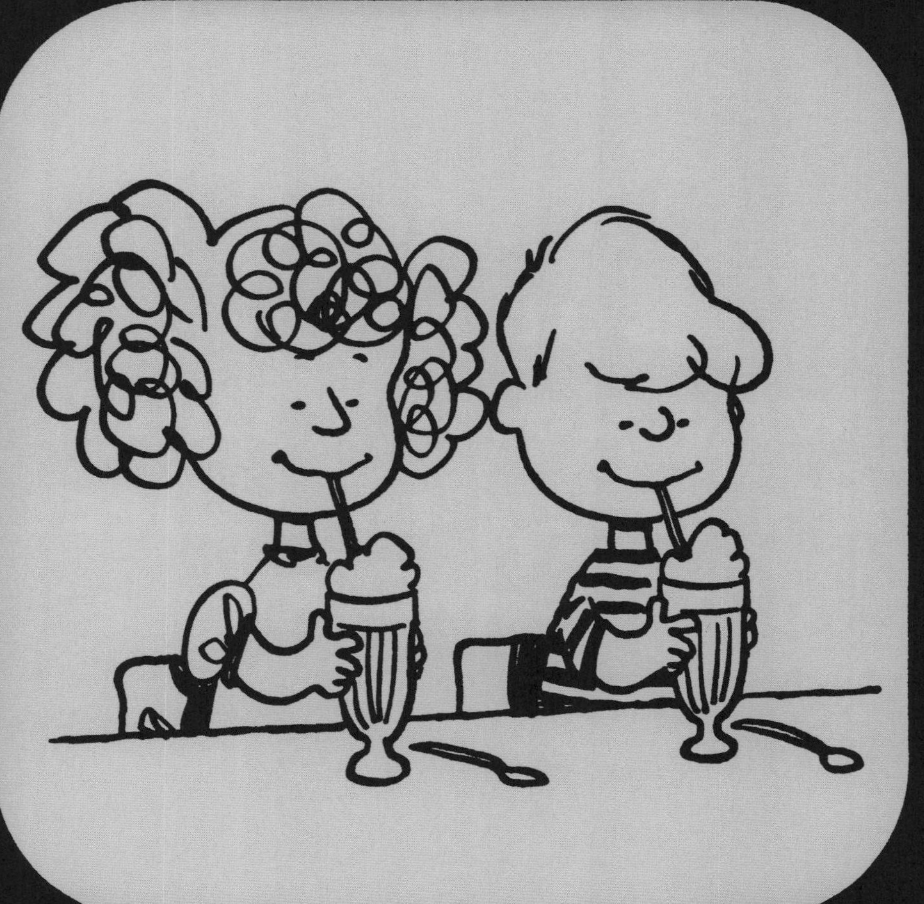

"A friend is someone who understands why you like your strawberry sodas without any strawberries in them."

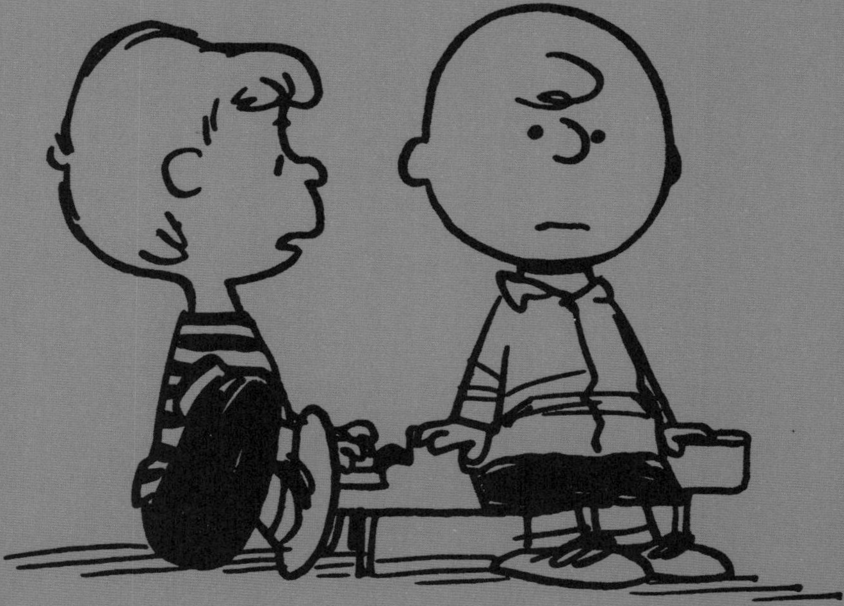

"A friend
is someone
you have things
in common with,
Charlie Brown."

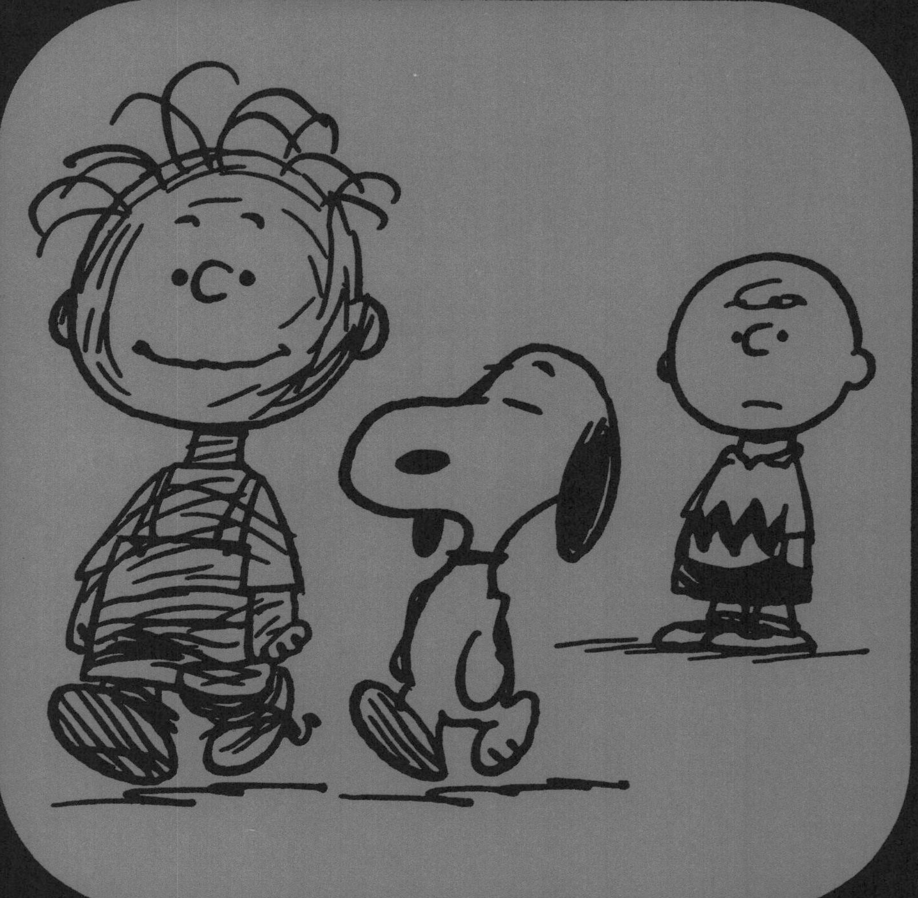

"A friend
is someone
who is not jealous
if you have
other friends."

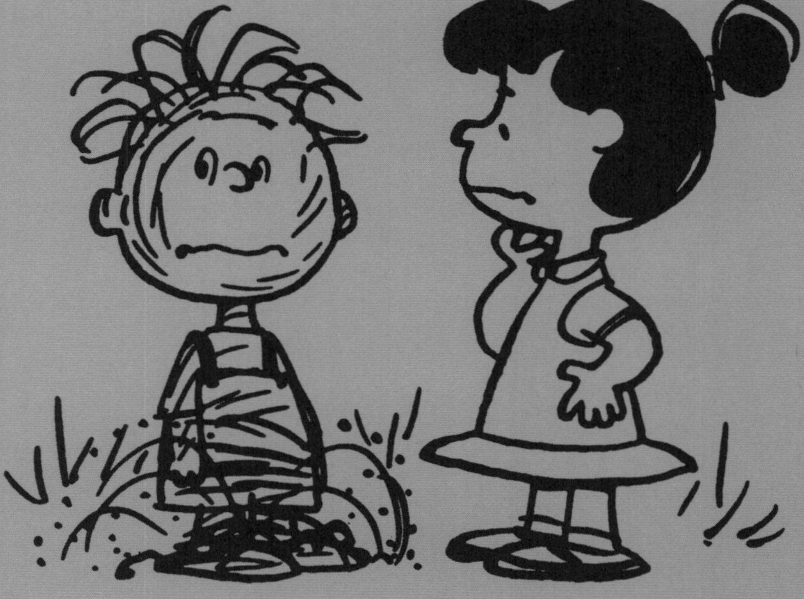

"A friend is someone who accepts you for what you are."

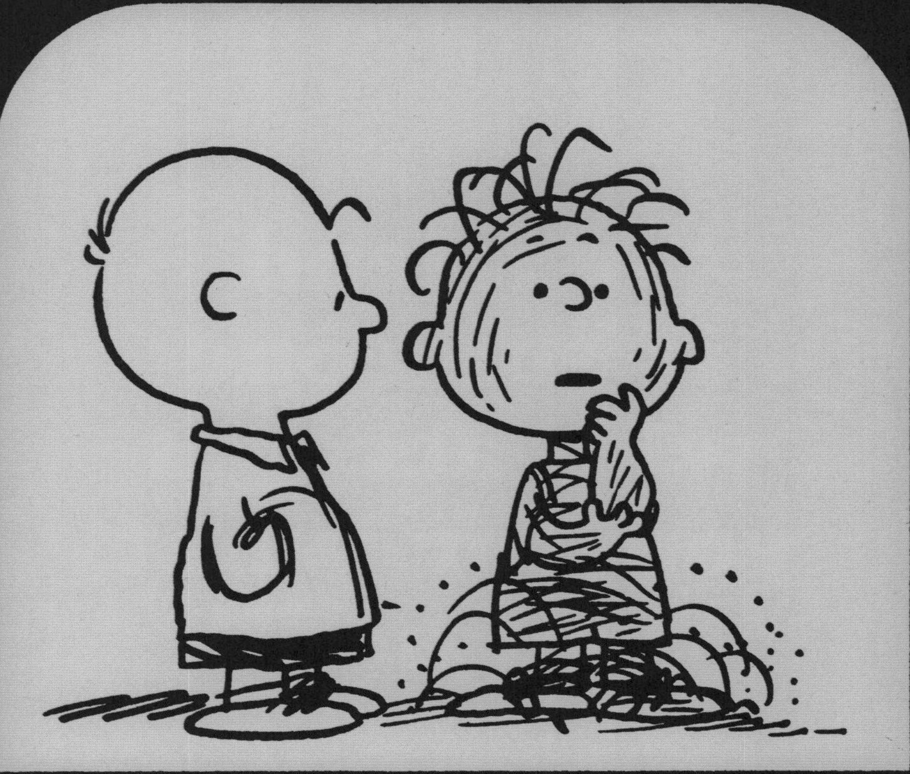

"You know what I think
a friend is, Charlie Brown?"

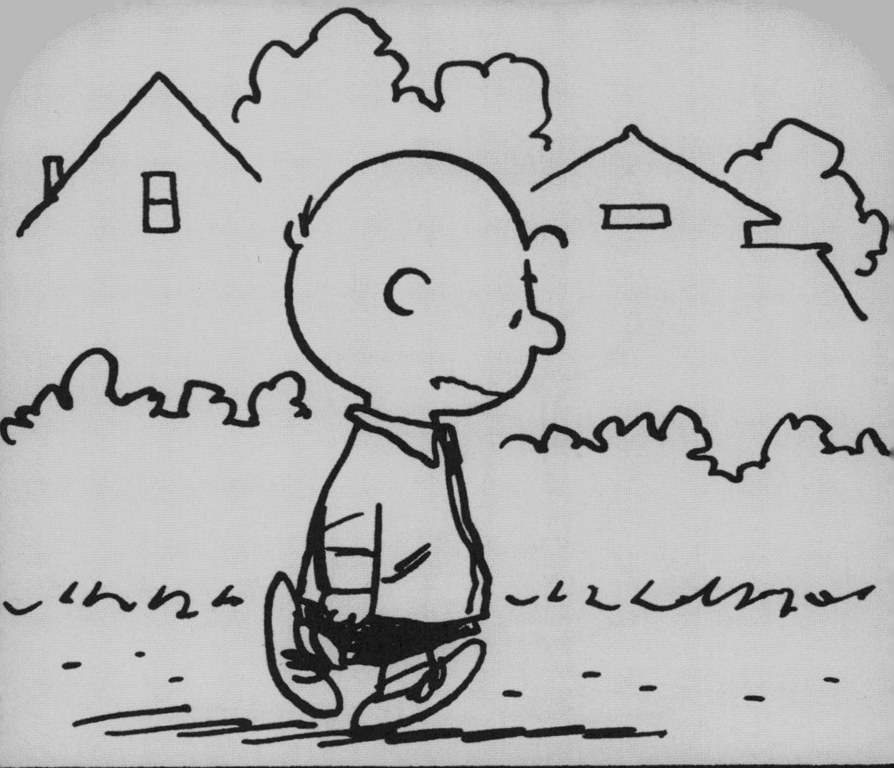

"I don't know...Talking to her never does much for me..."

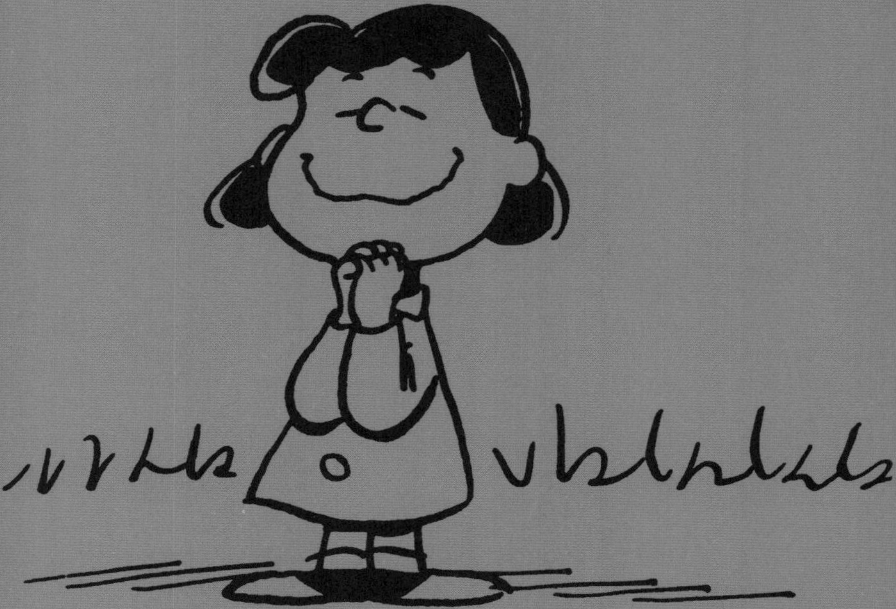

"Just so
I'm popular!"

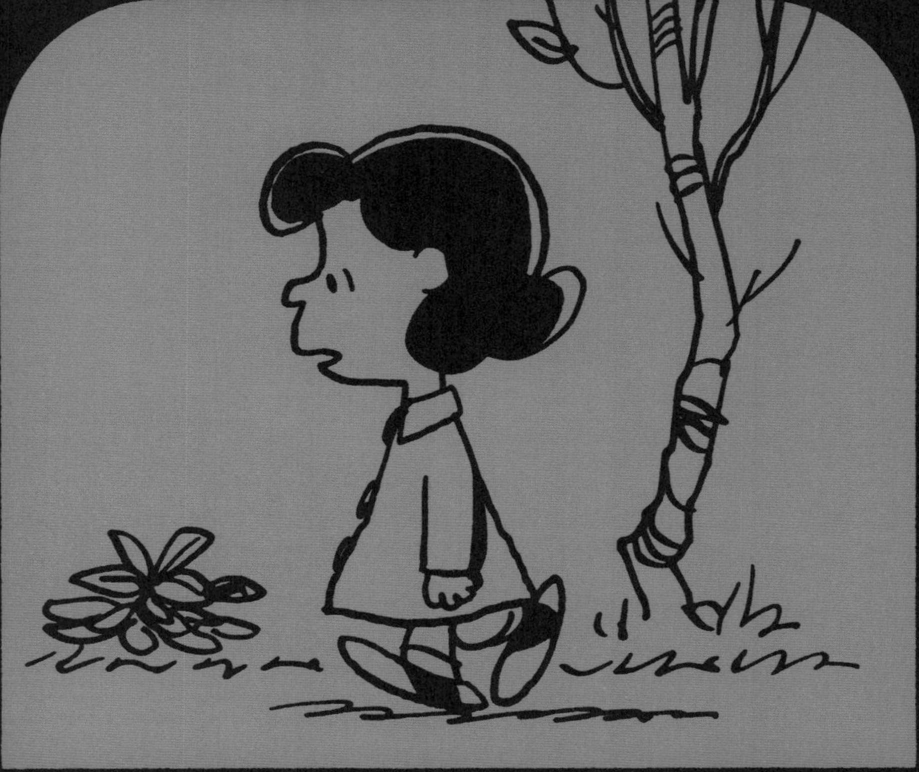

"Poor ol' Charlie Brown . . .
He really should try to be like me.
I don't care if I have any friends or not . . ."

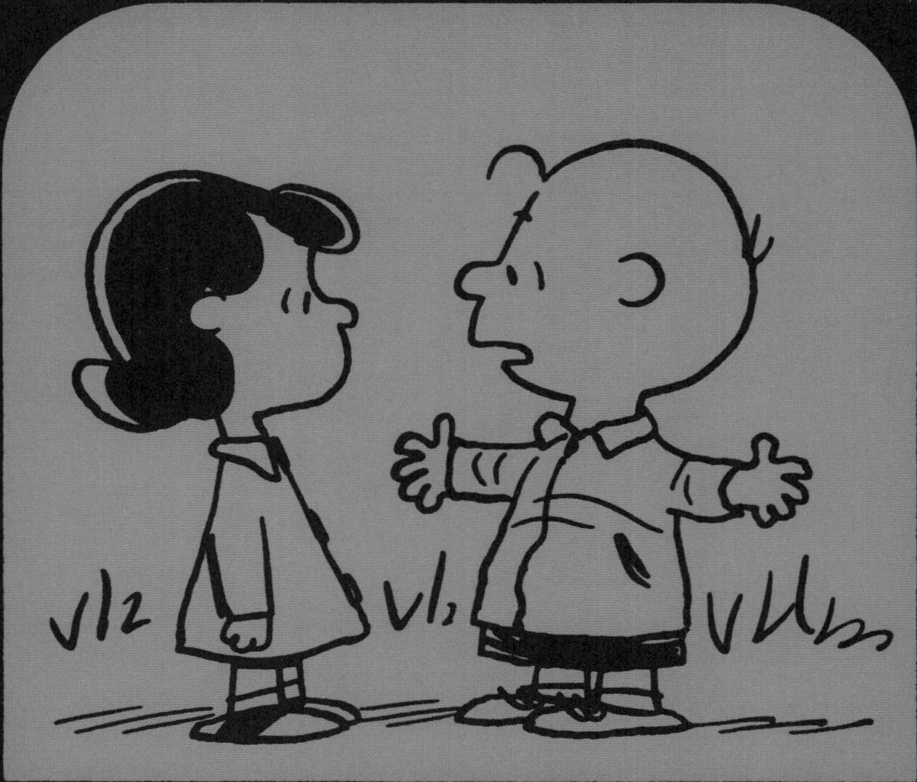

"I'd even settle for a 'fair-weather' friend!"

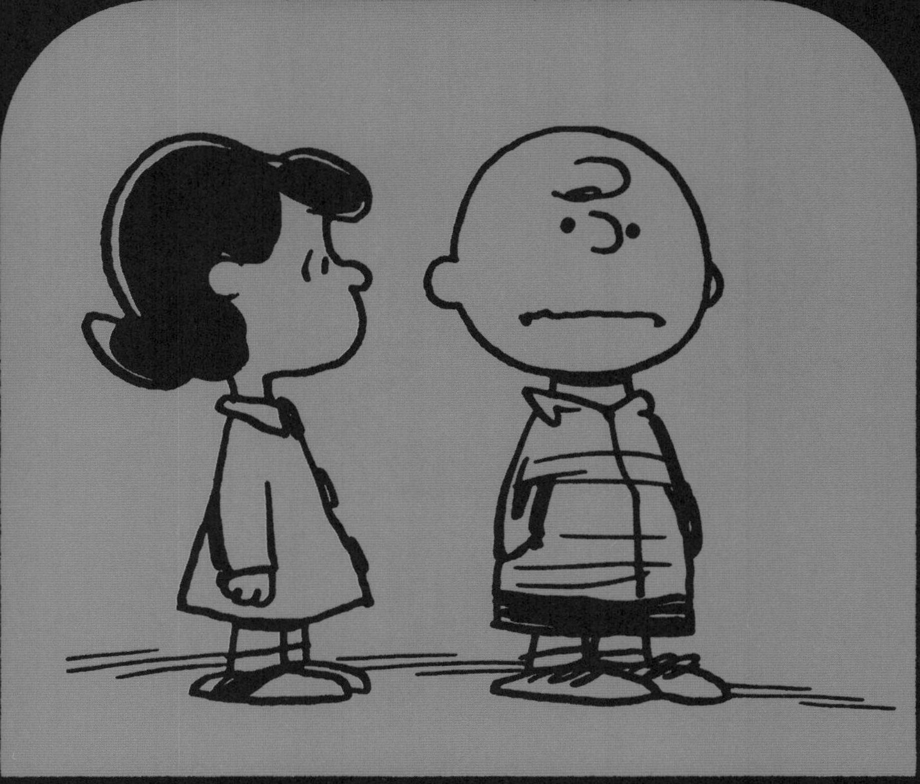

"Not me . . . I need all the friends I can get!"

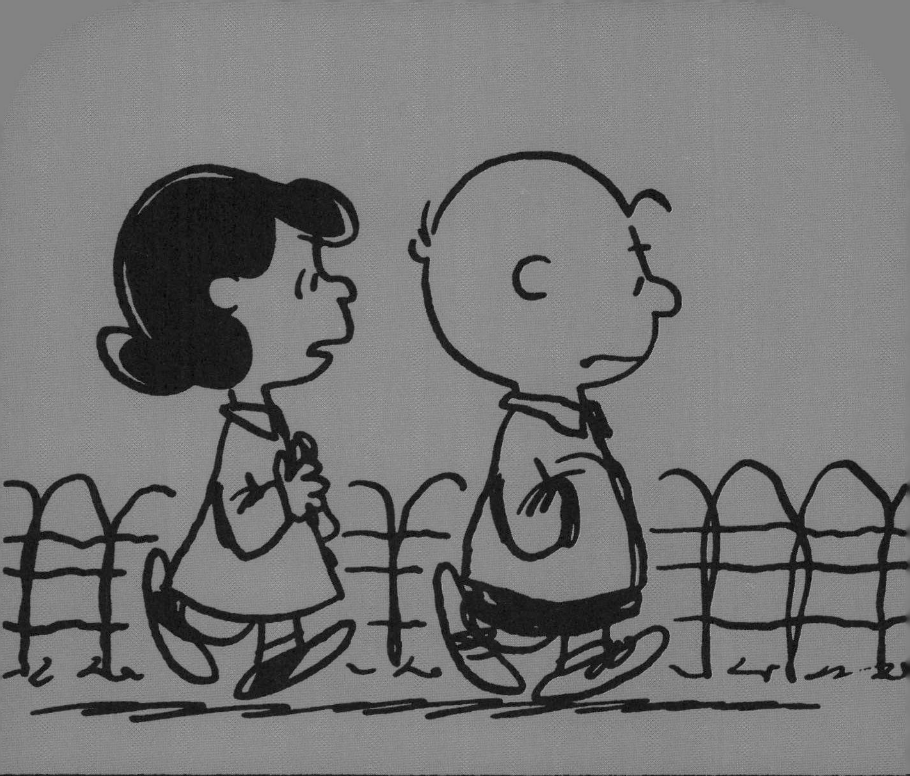

I think you try too hard, Charlie Brown . . .
Be like me. I don't need any friends . . .

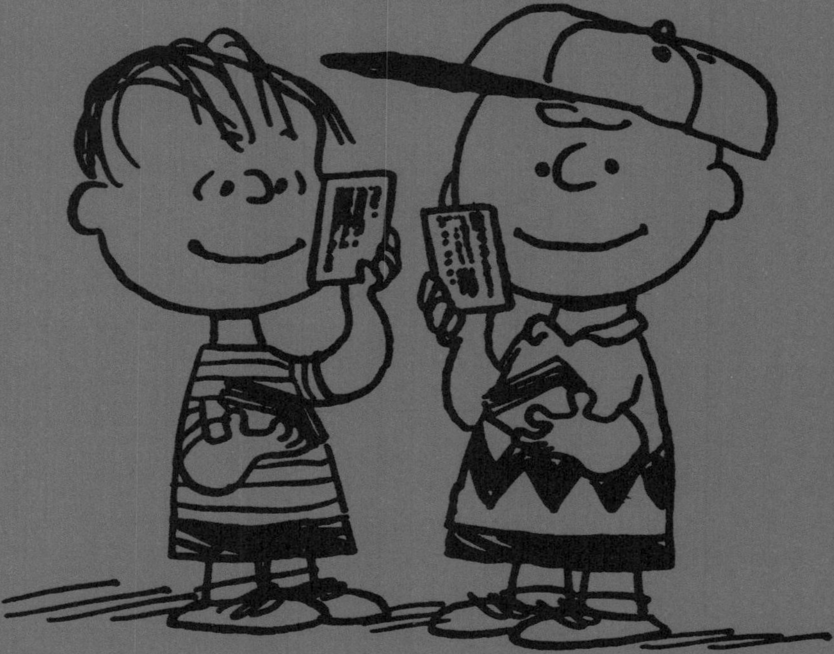

"A friend is someone who will trade you an Alvin Dark for a Luis Aparicio."

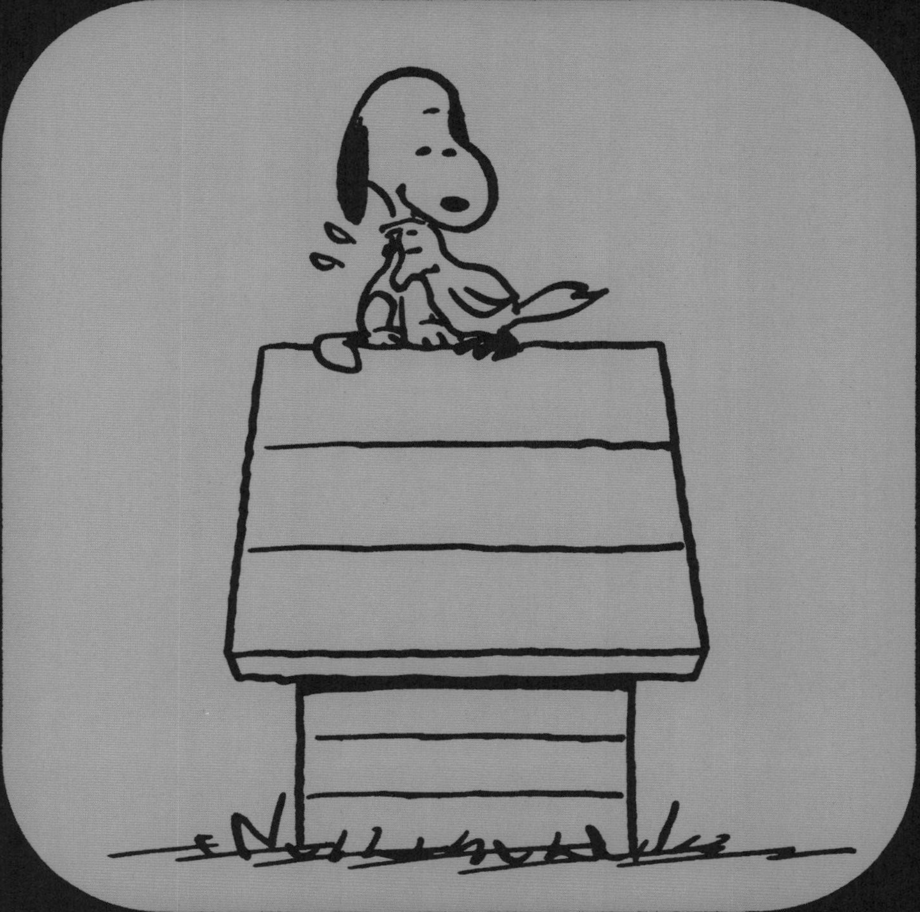

"A friend is someone who will share his home with you."

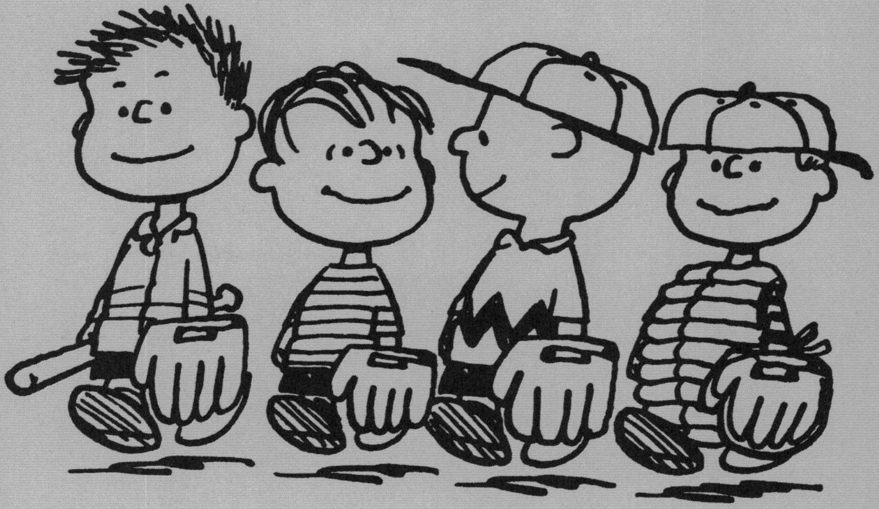

"A friend is someone who likes you even when the other guys are around."

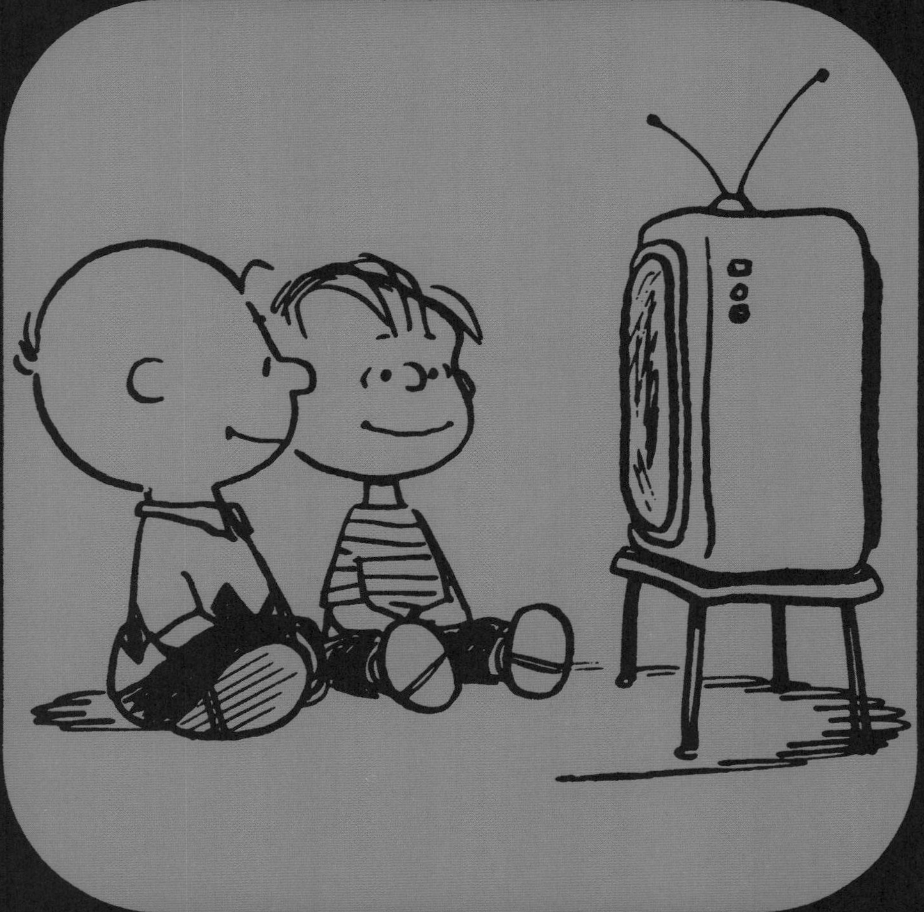

"A friend
is someone
who's willing to
watch the program
you want to
watch!"

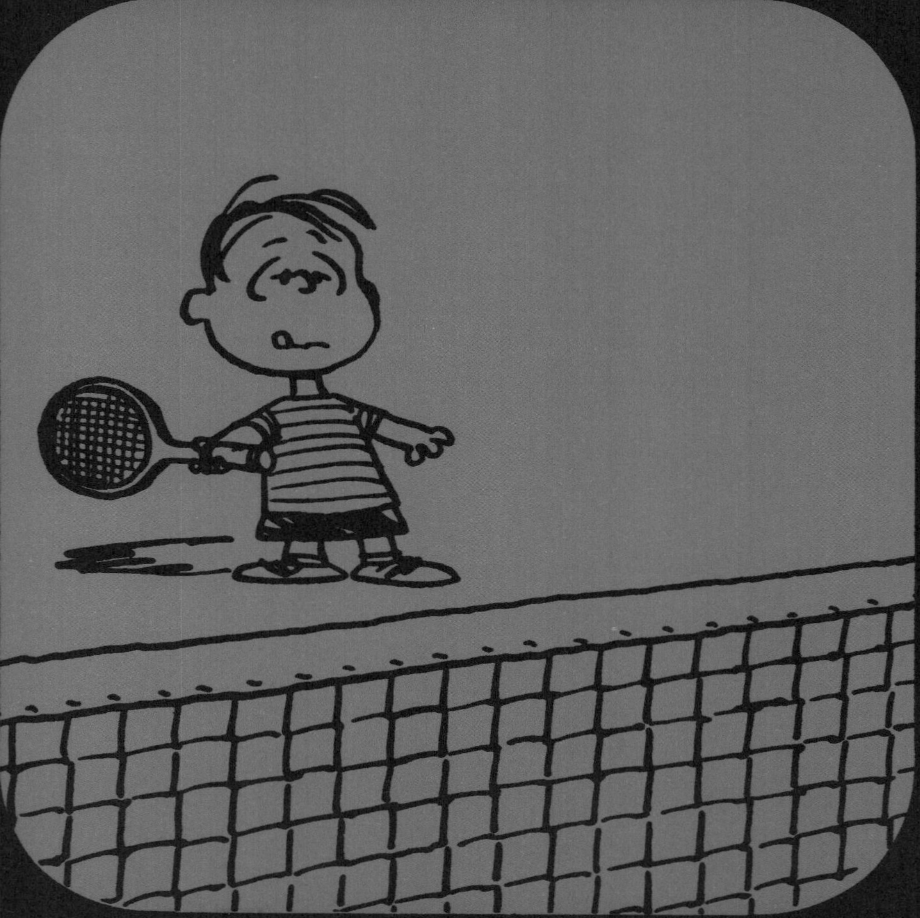

"A friend is someone who will take the side with the sun in his eyes."

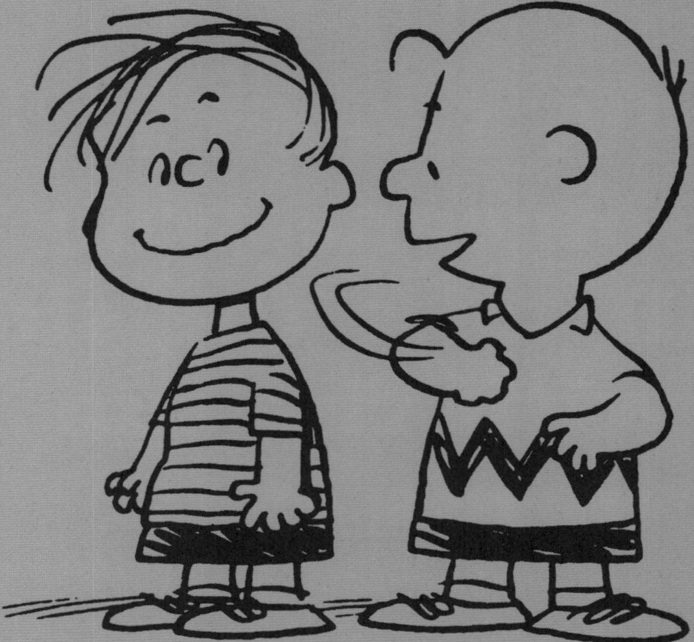

"A friend is someone you can sock on the arm!"

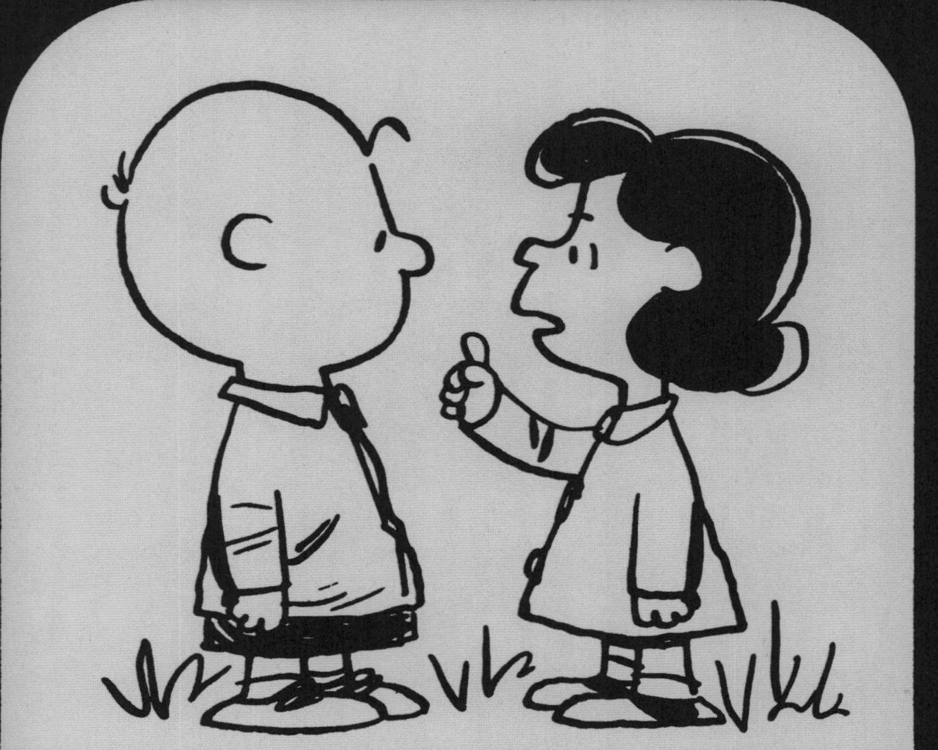

"'Define 'Friend'!"

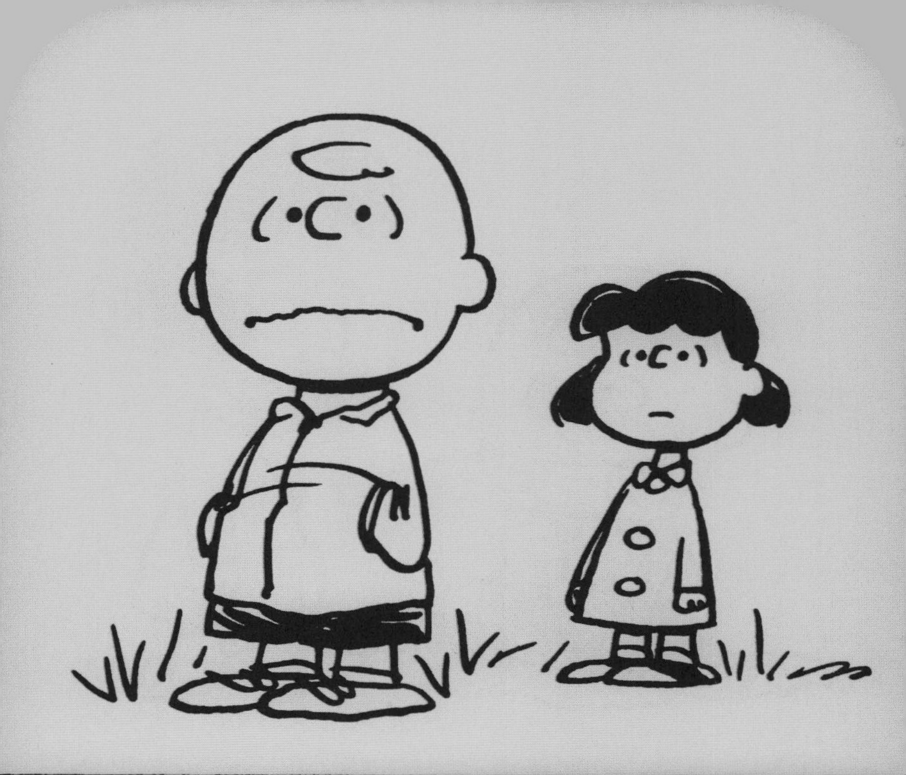

"I don't have any friends . . . I don't have one single person I can call a friend."

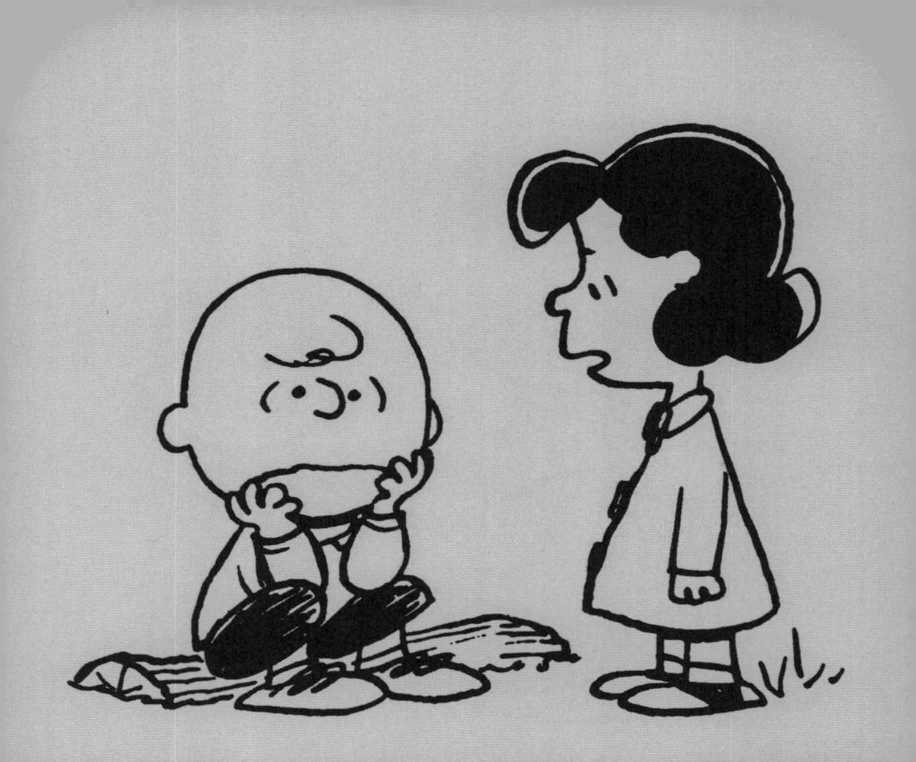

'What's the matter with you?'

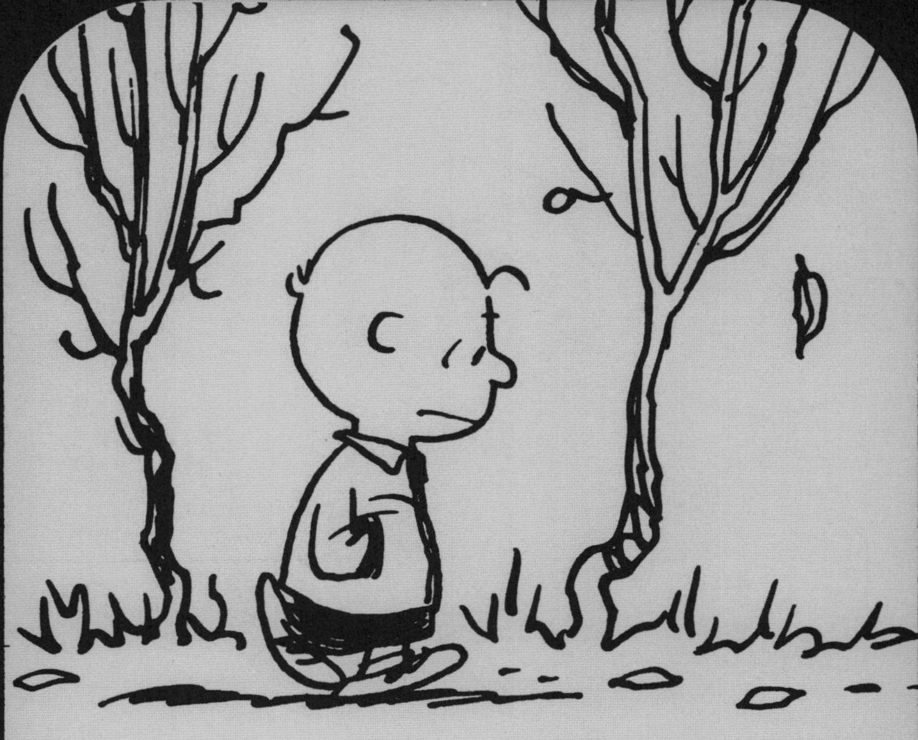

"Nobody likes me . . .
Nobody cares if I live or die!"

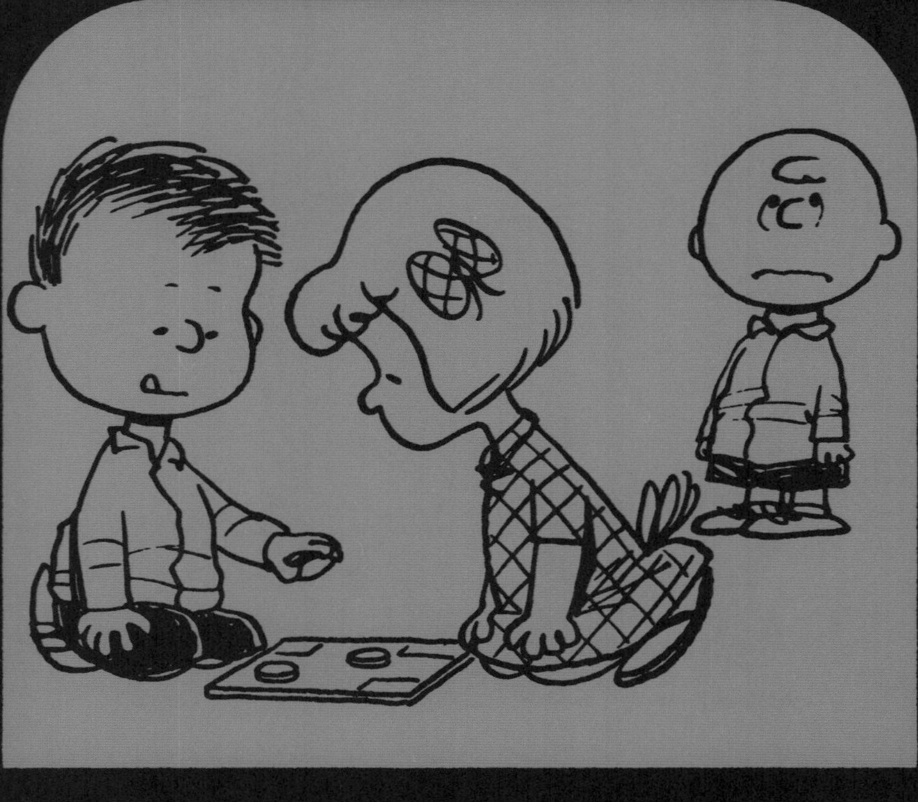

"Sigh!"

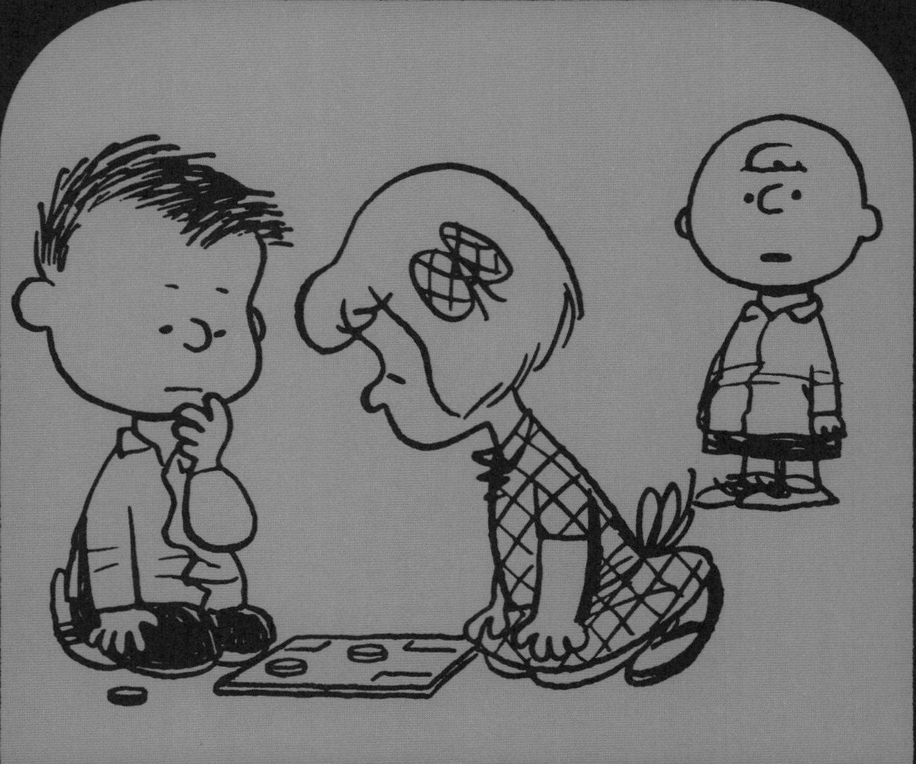

"I said, I hate to spoil all the fun, but I have to be going."

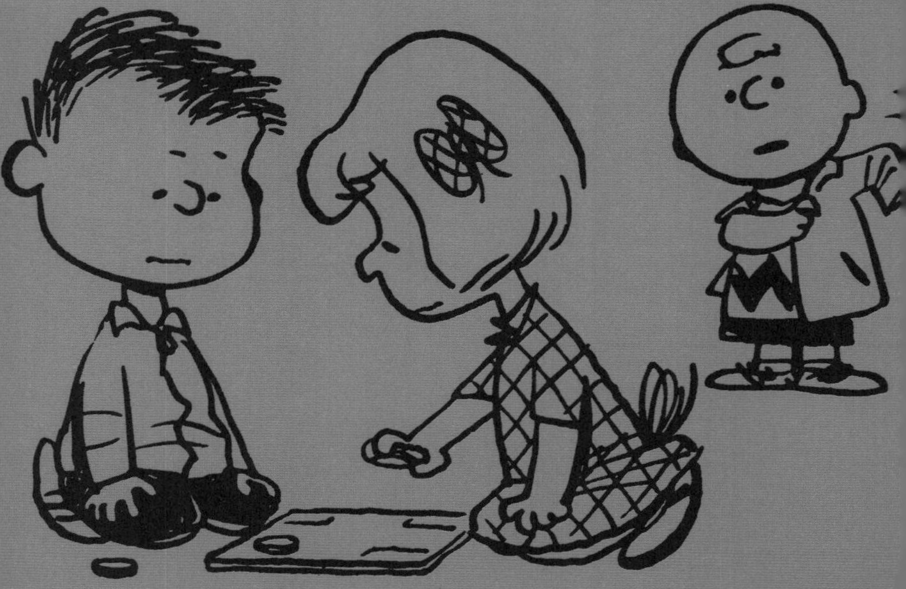

"Well,
I hate
to spoil all
the fun, but I
have to be
going."

I NEED ALL THE FRIENDS I CAN GET

PENGUIN WORKSHOP
An imprint of Penguin Random House LLC

This edition published by Penguin Workshop, an imprint of Penguin Random House LLC, New York, 2022

PEANUTS and all related titles, logos and characters are trademarks of Peanuts Worldwide LLC

© 1964 Peanuts Worldwide LLC. Originally published 1964.

Penguin supports copyright. Copyright fuels creativity, encourages diverse voices,
promotes free speech, and creates a vibrant culture. Thank you for buying an authorized edition
of this book and for complying with copyright laws by not reproducing, scanning, or distributing
any part of it in any form without permission. You are supporting writers and allowing
Penguin to continue to publish books for every reader.

PENGUIN is a registered trademark and PENGUIN WORKSHOP is a trademark of Penguin Books Ltd, and
the W colophon is a registered trademark of Penguin Random House LLC.

Visit us online at penguinrandomhouse.com.

Library of Congress Cataloging-in-Publication Data is available.

Manufactured in China

ISBN 9780593519677   10 9 8 7 6 5 4 3 2 TOPL

I NEED ALL THE FRIENDS I CAN GET

BY

CHARLES M. SCHULZ

TO:

_____

FROM:

_____

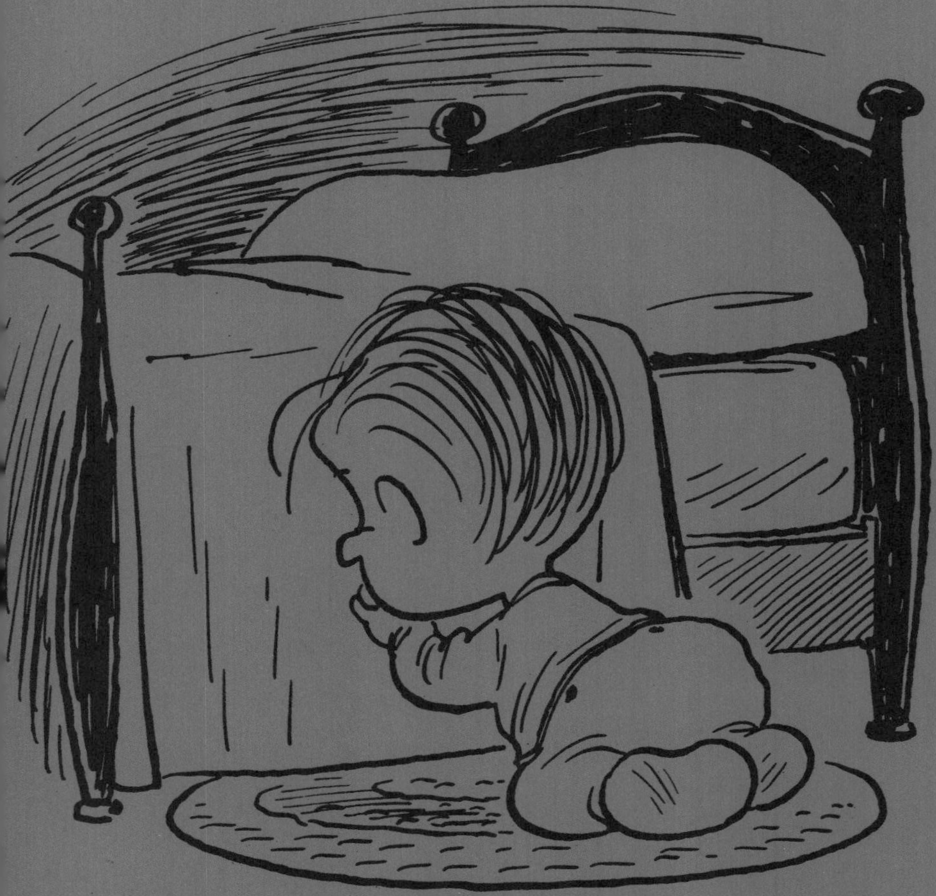

Security is knowing you're not alone.

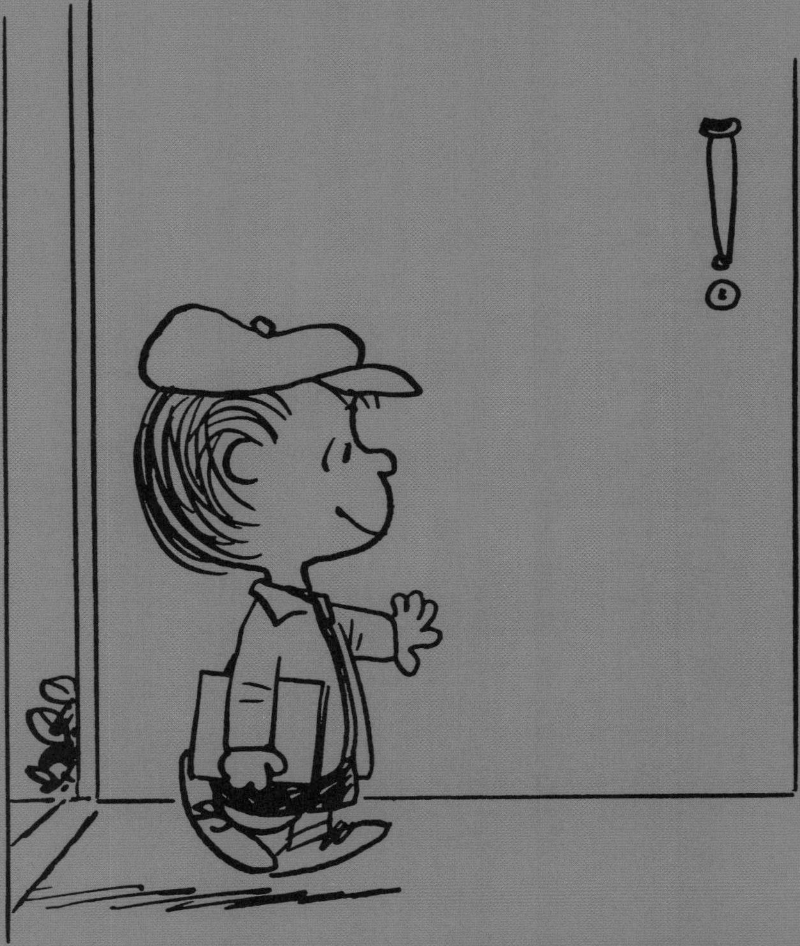
!

**Security
is hearing
your mother
in the kitchen
when you
come home
from school.**

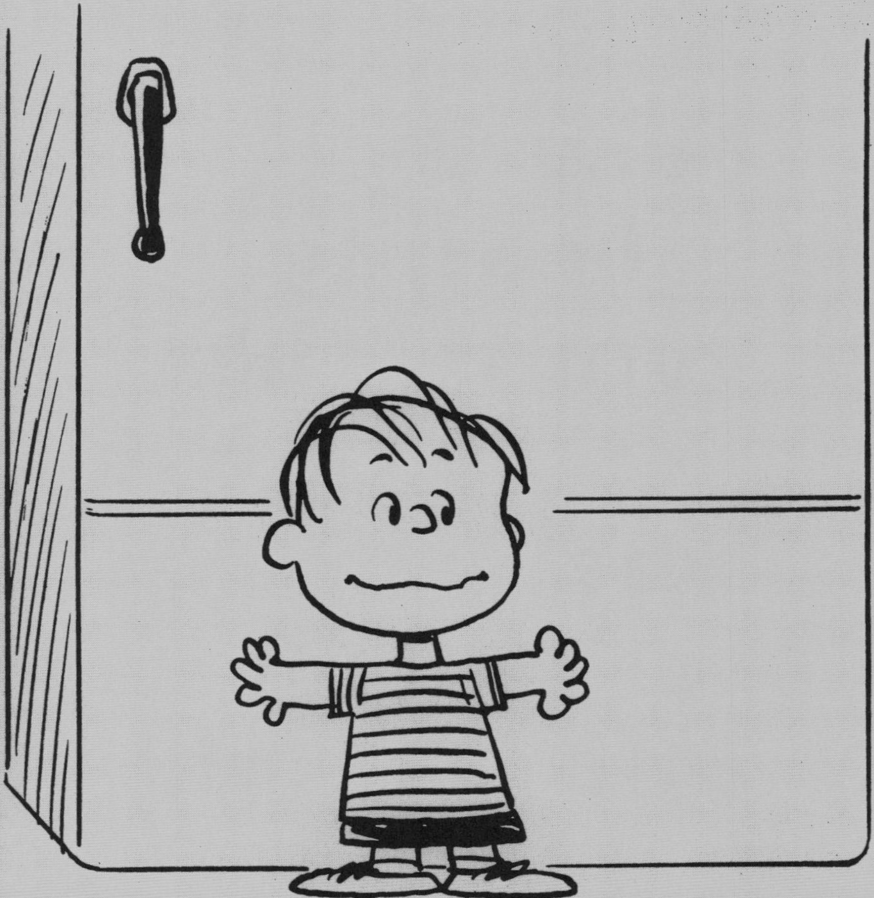

Security is a candy bar hidden in the freezer.

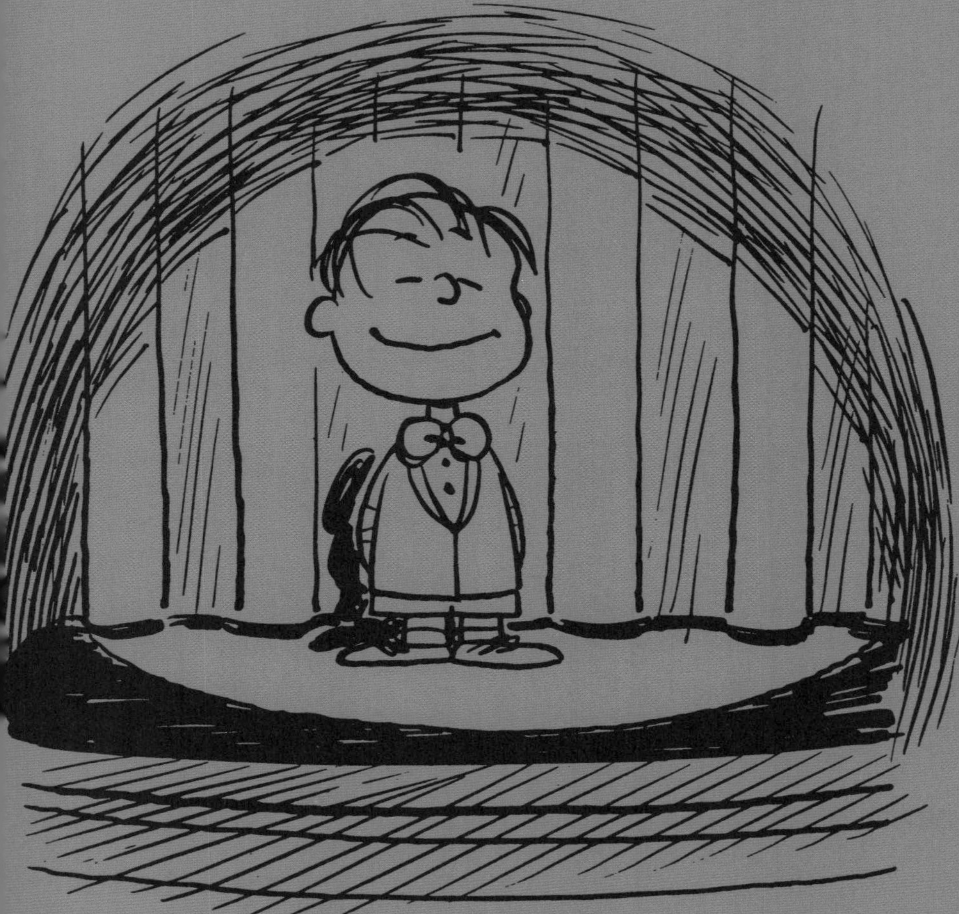

Security
is knowing
all your
lines.

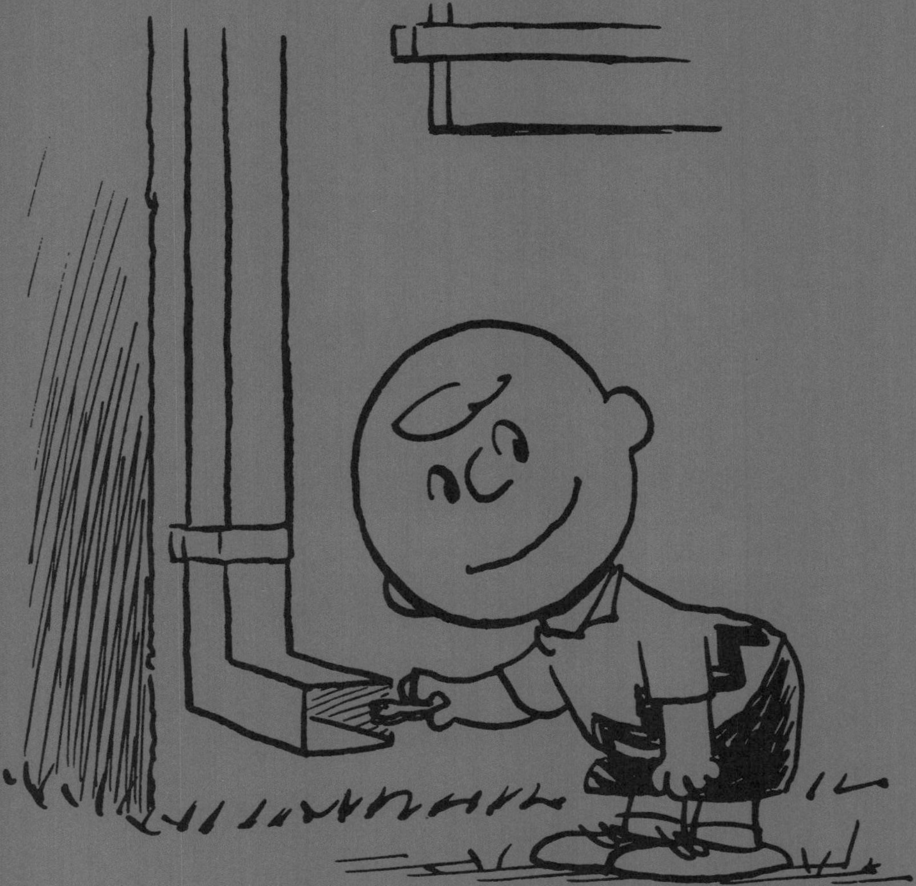

Security is hiding an extra key to the back door.

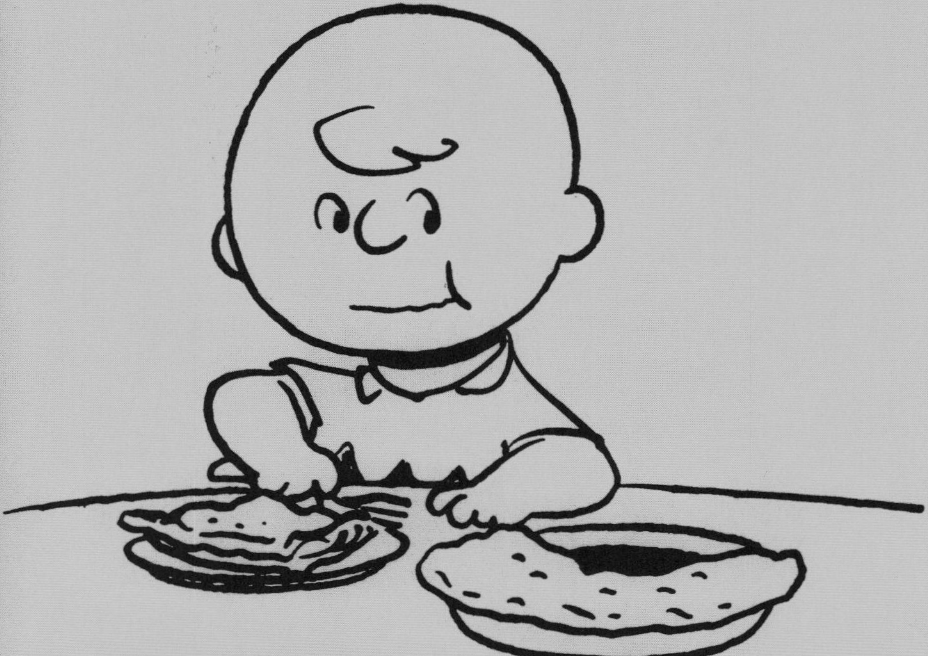

Security
is knowing
there's
some more
pie left.

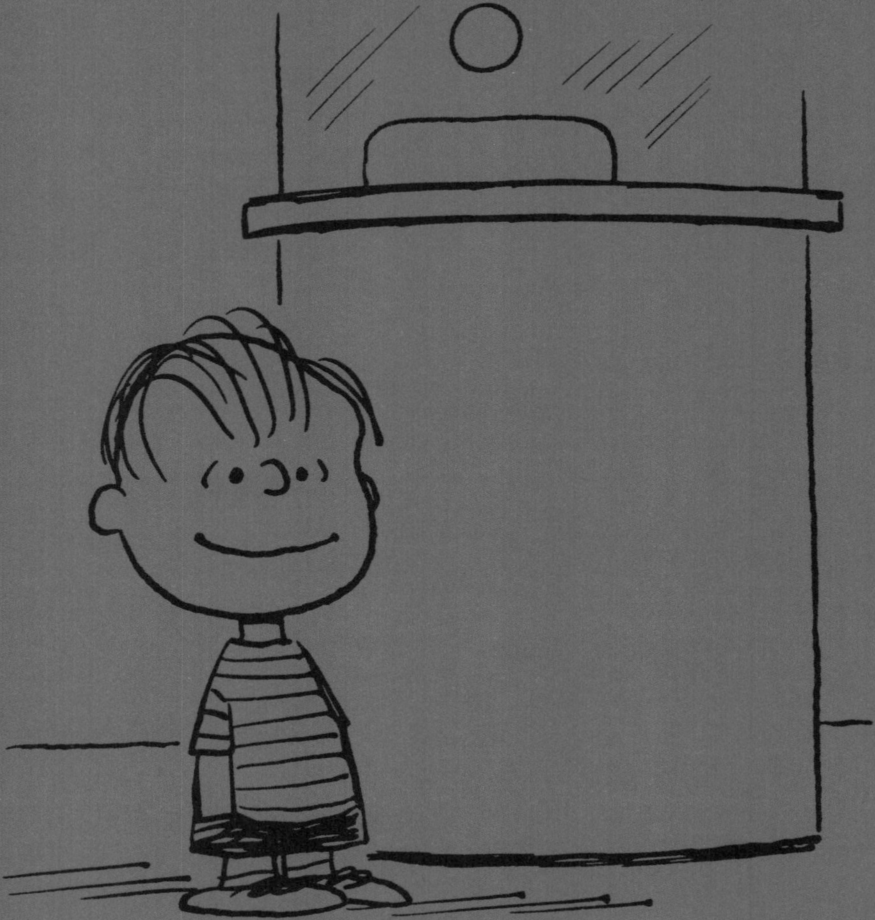

**Security
is getting
to the theater
before the
box office
opens.**

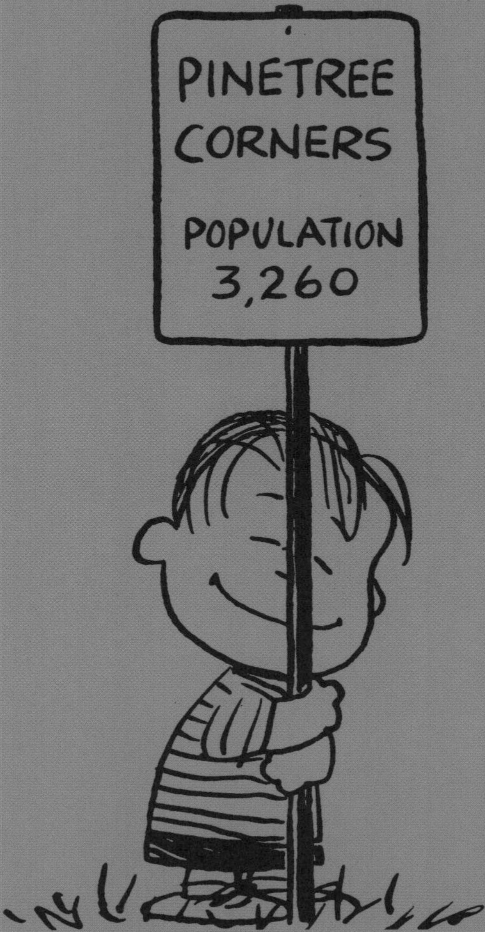
PINETREE
CORNERS
POPULATION
3,260

Security is having a home town.

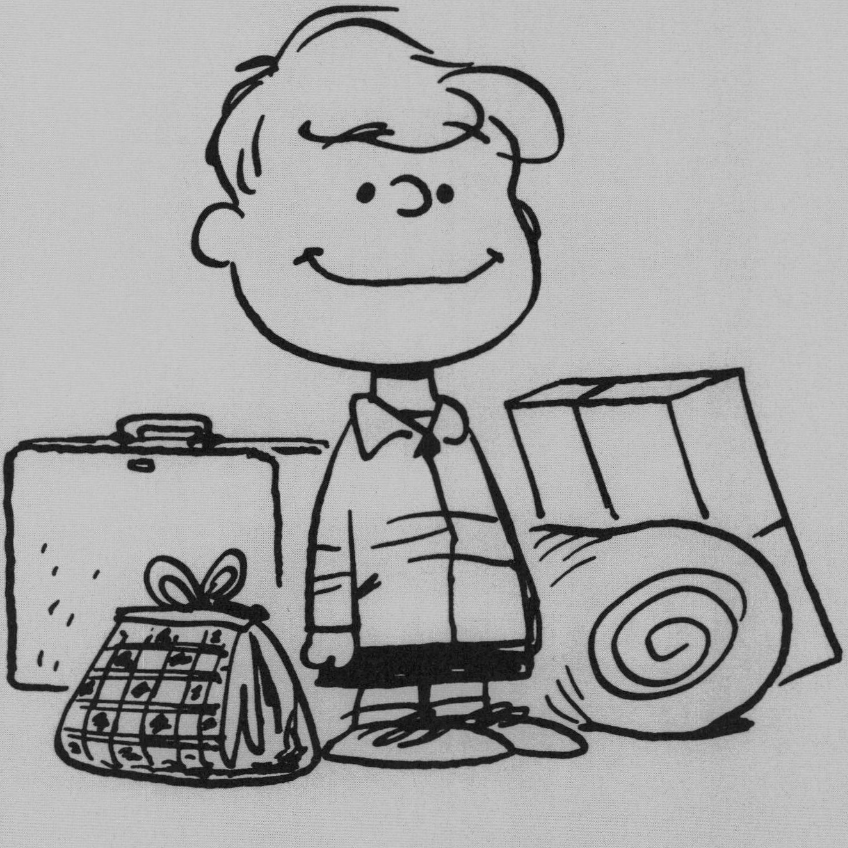

Security is returning home after a vacation.

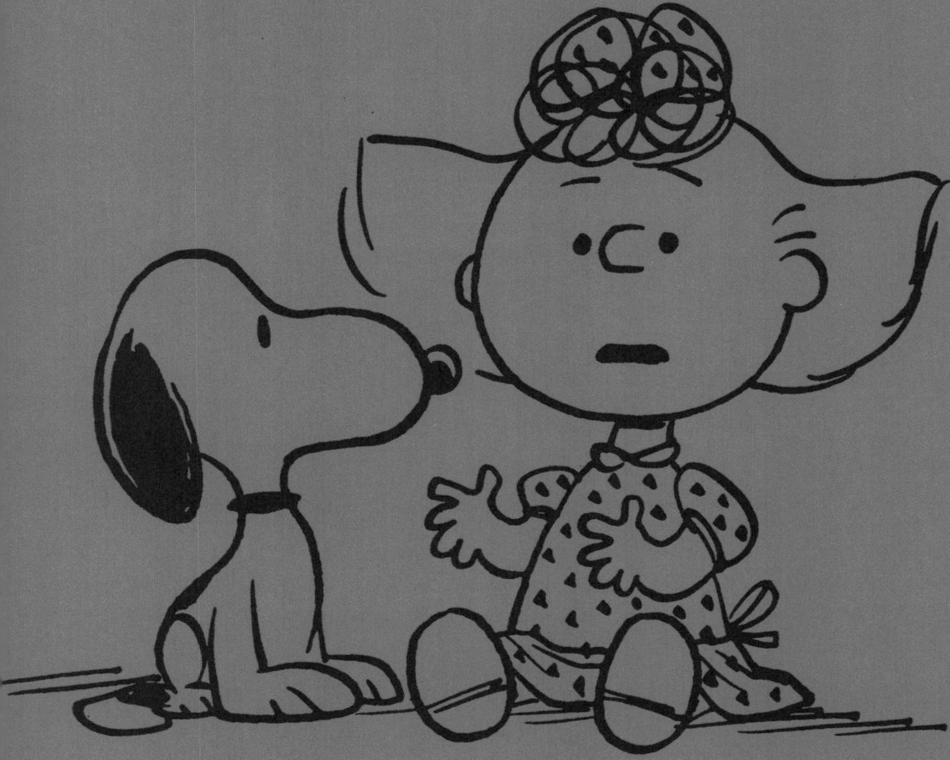

Security is having someone listen to you.

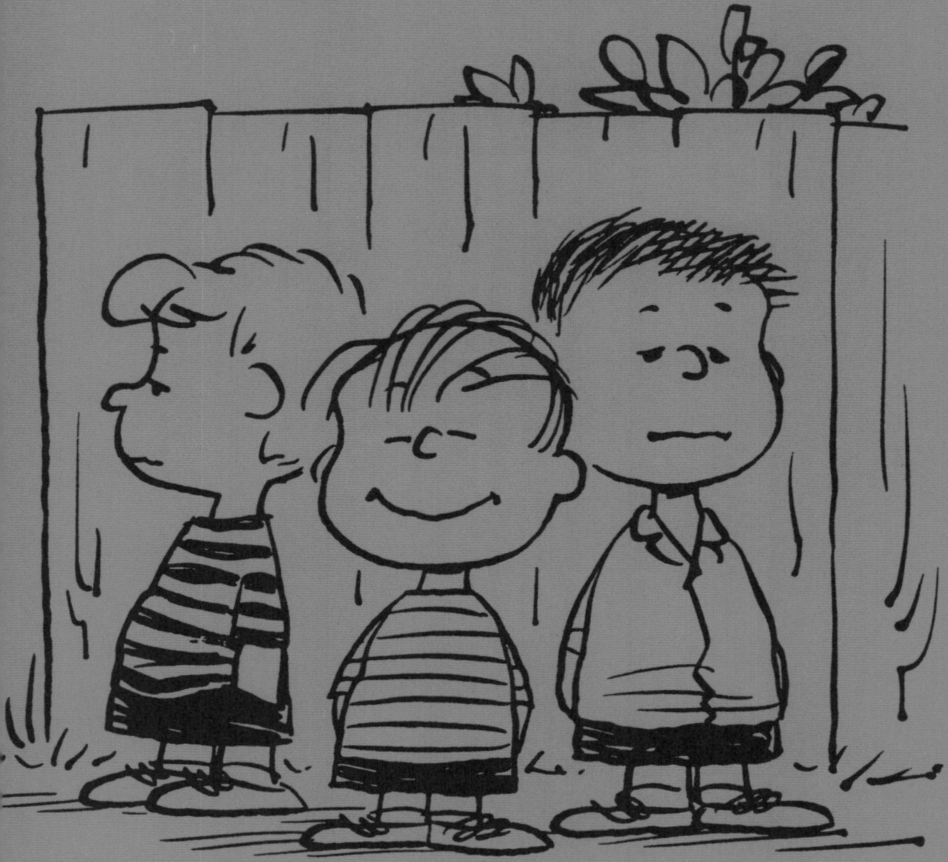

Security
is being
one of
the gang.

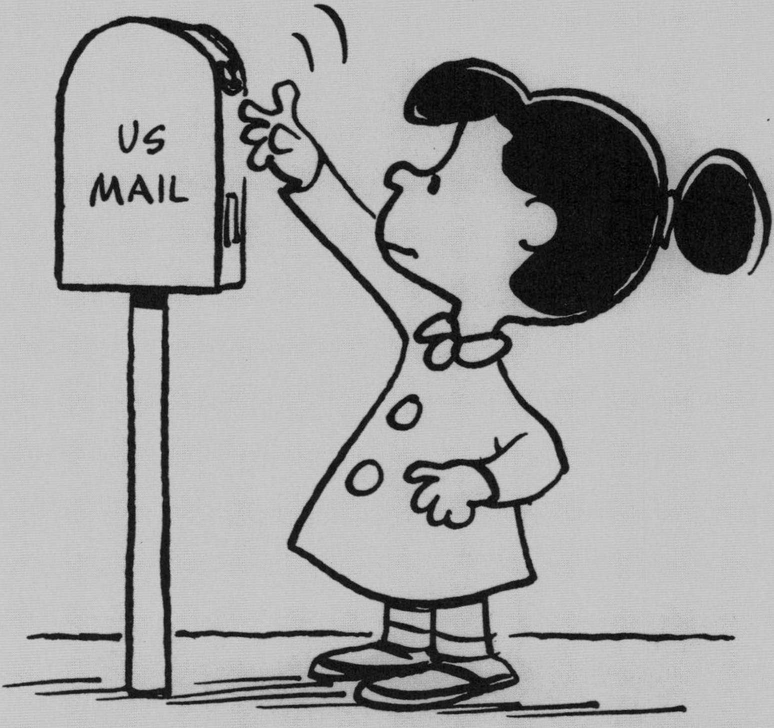
US MAIL

Security is giving the mailbox lid an extra flip.

Security is being able to touch bottom.

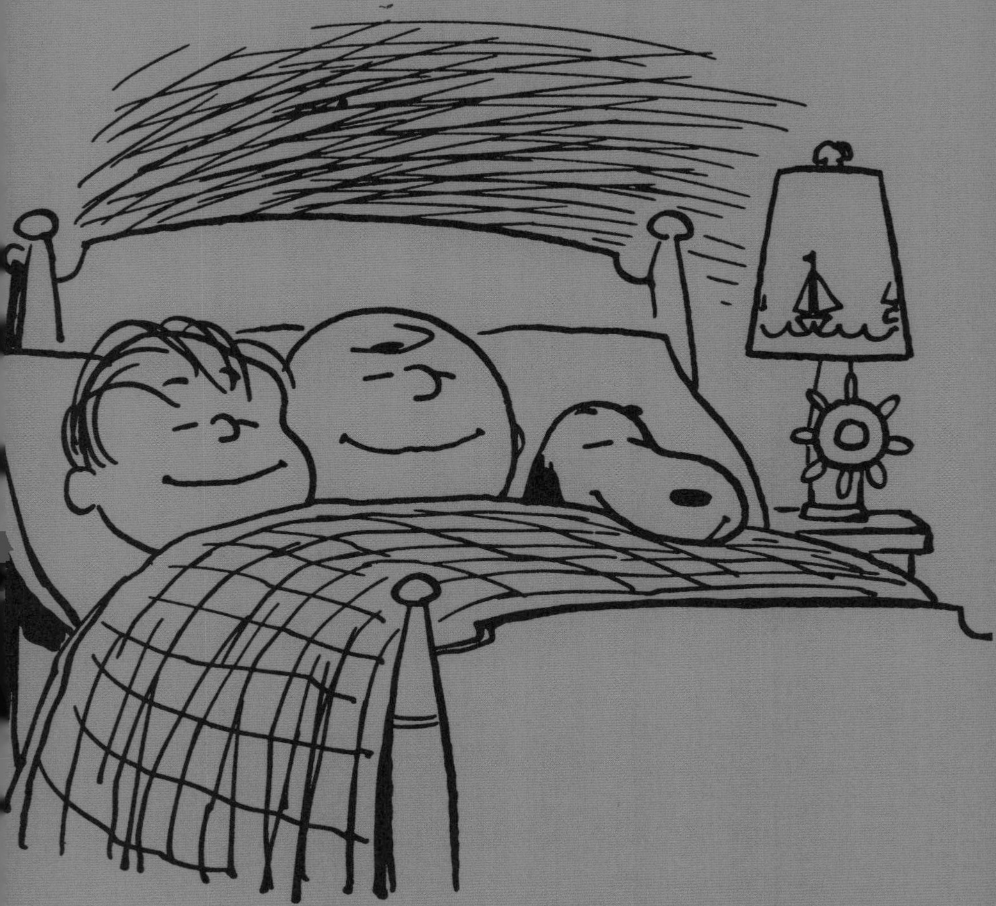

**Security
is having
some friends
sleep
overnight.**

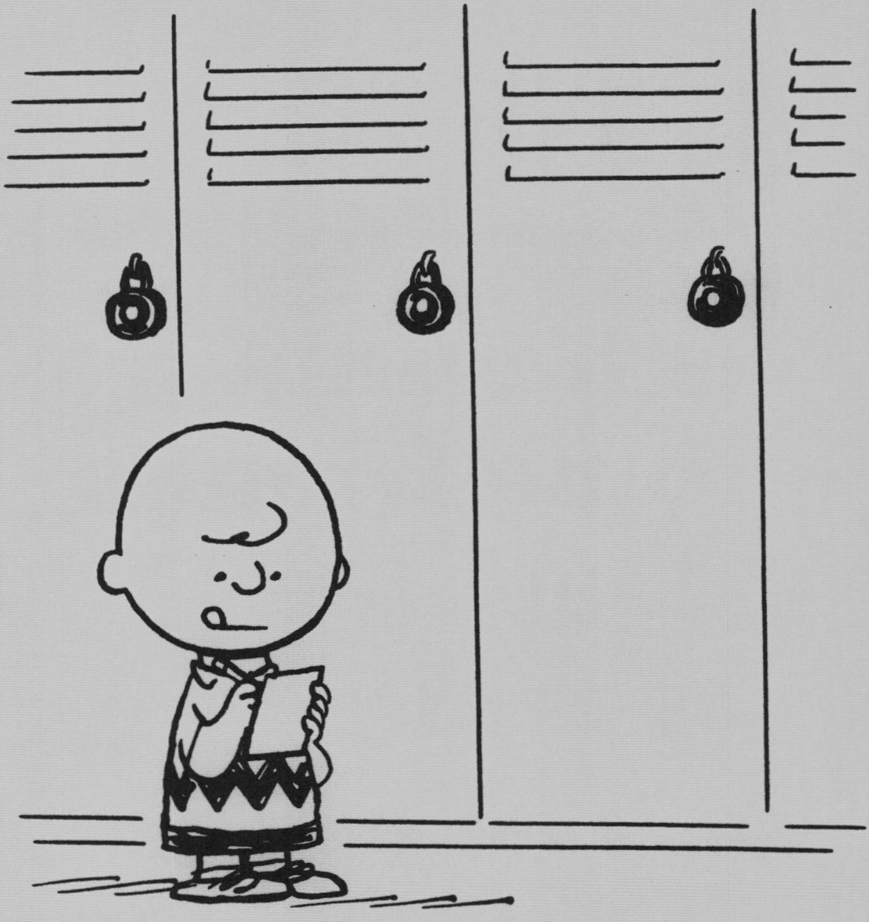

Security is writing down your locker combination.

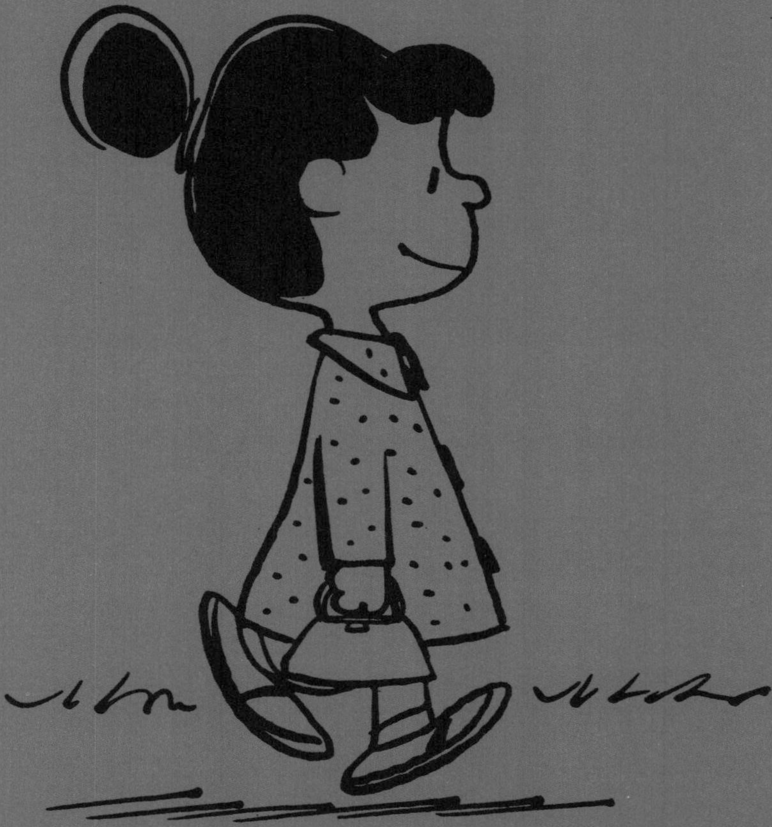

Security is carrying an extra safety pin in your purse.

Security is holding the tickets in your hand.

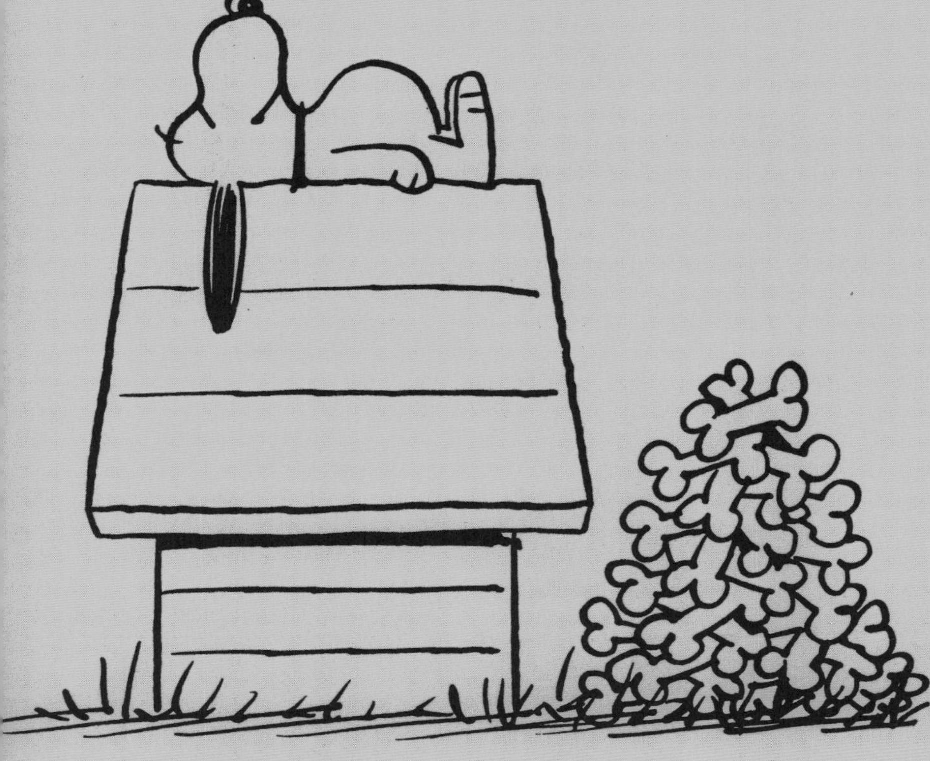

**Security
is having
a few bones
stacked
away.**

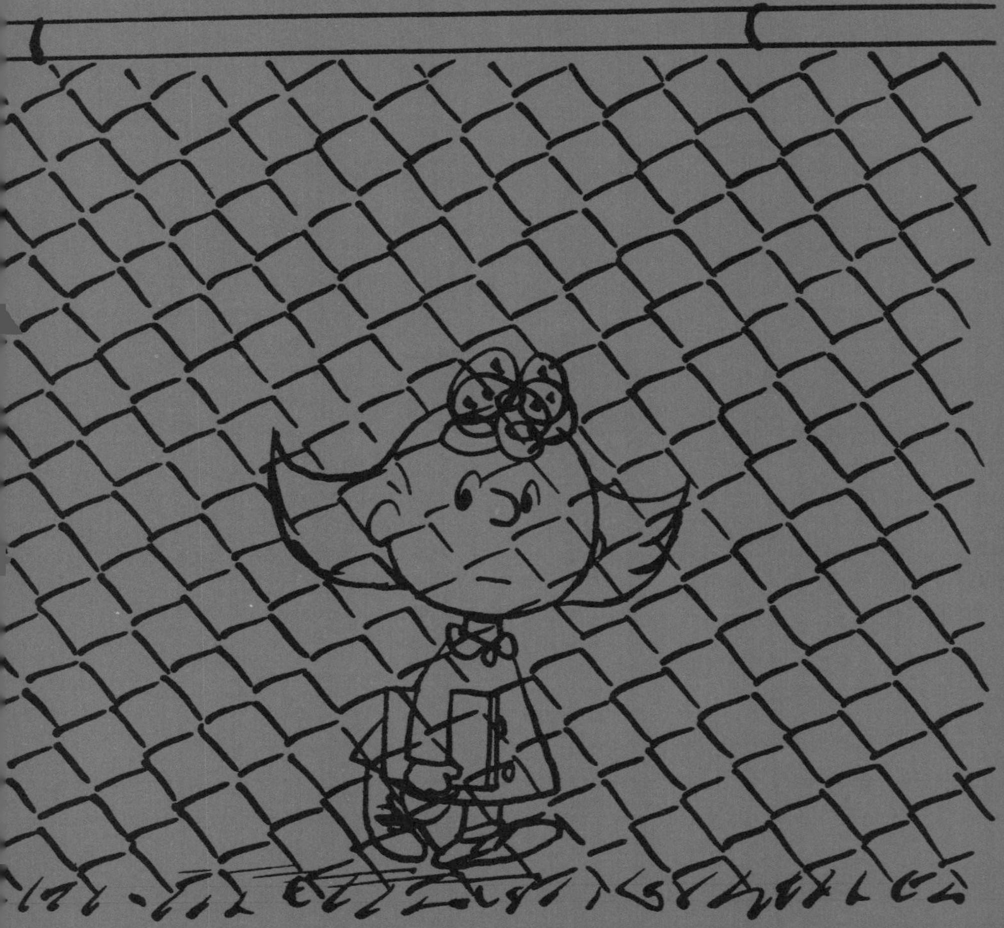

**Security
is knowing
that big dog
can't really
get out.**

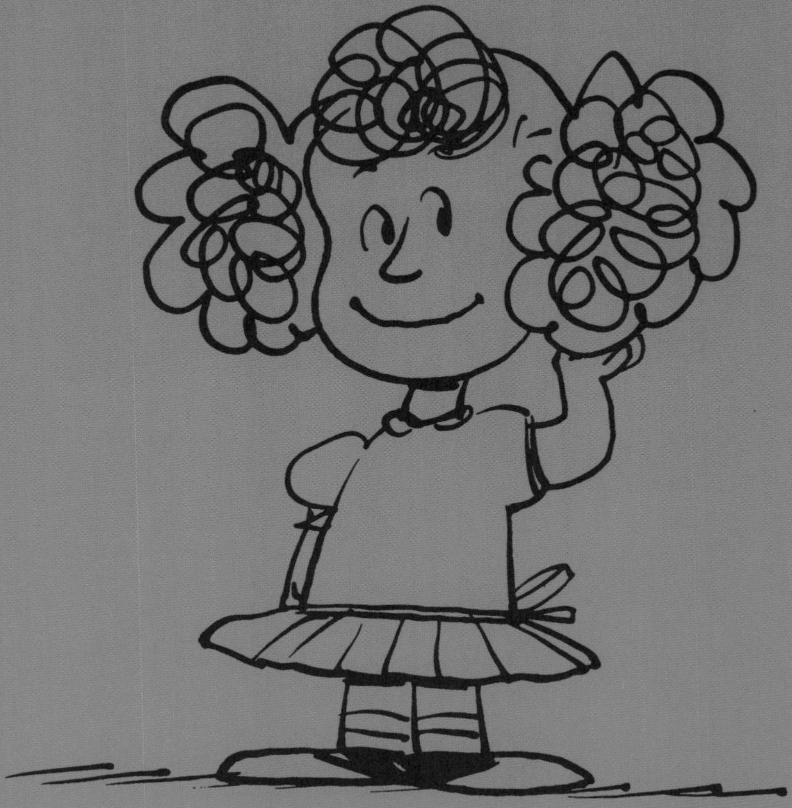

Security is having naturally curly hair.

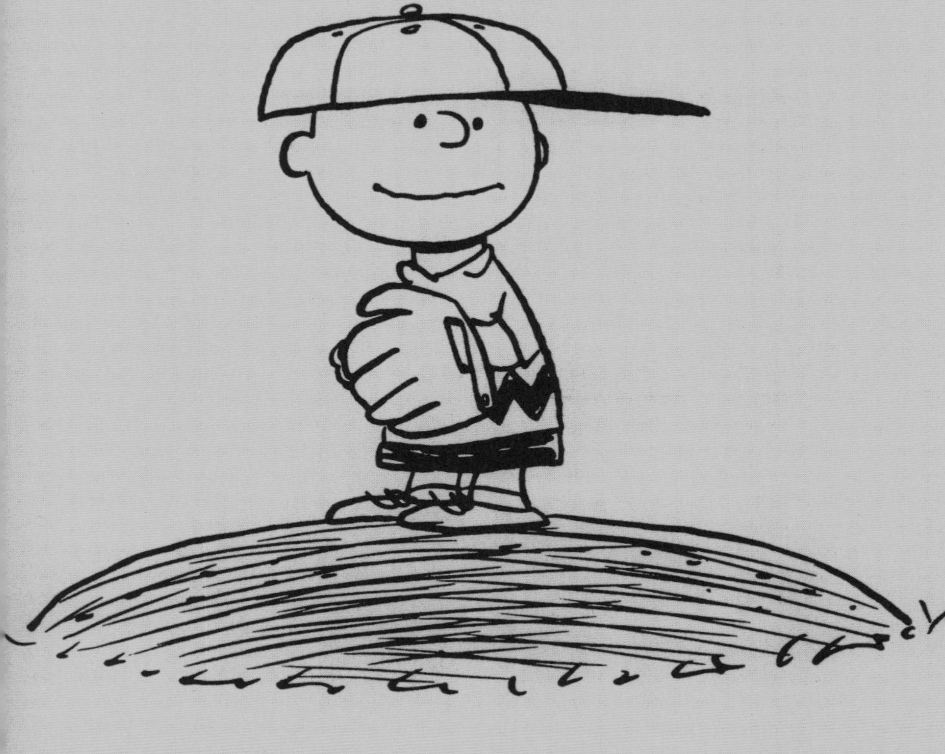

Security
is having a
good infield
behind you.

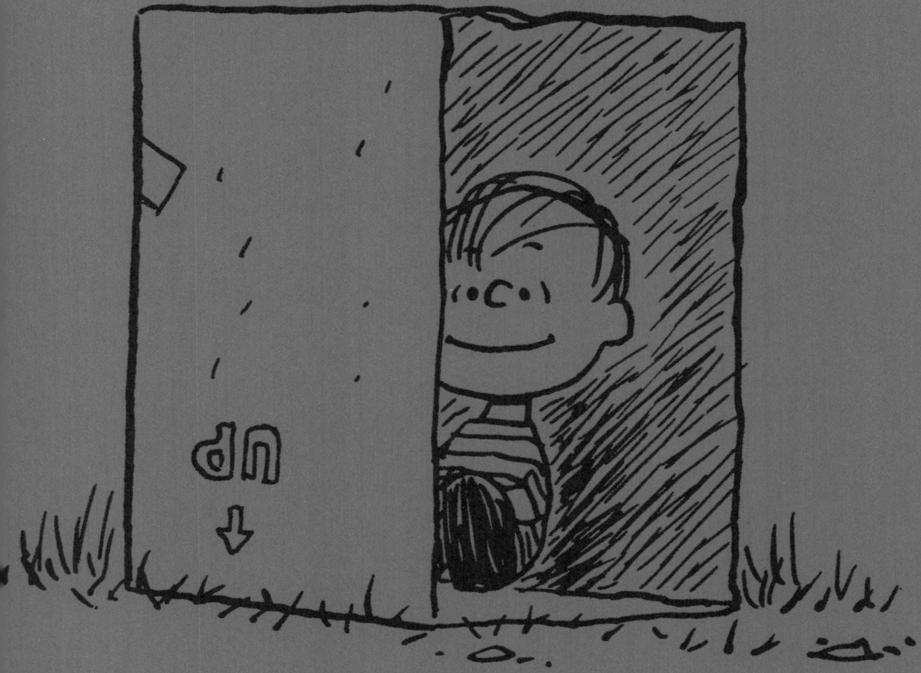

Security
is sitting
in a box.

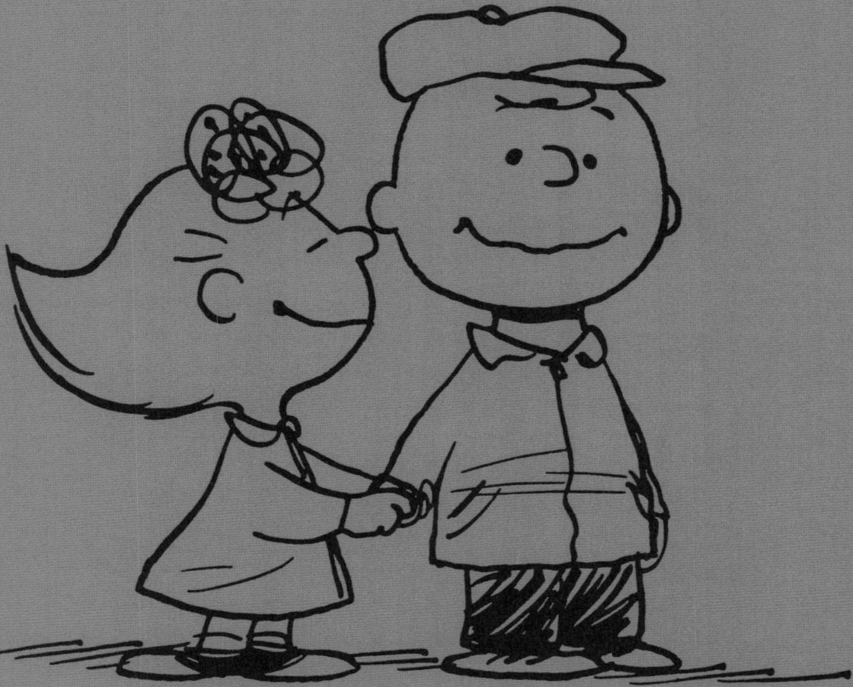

Security
is having
a big
brother.

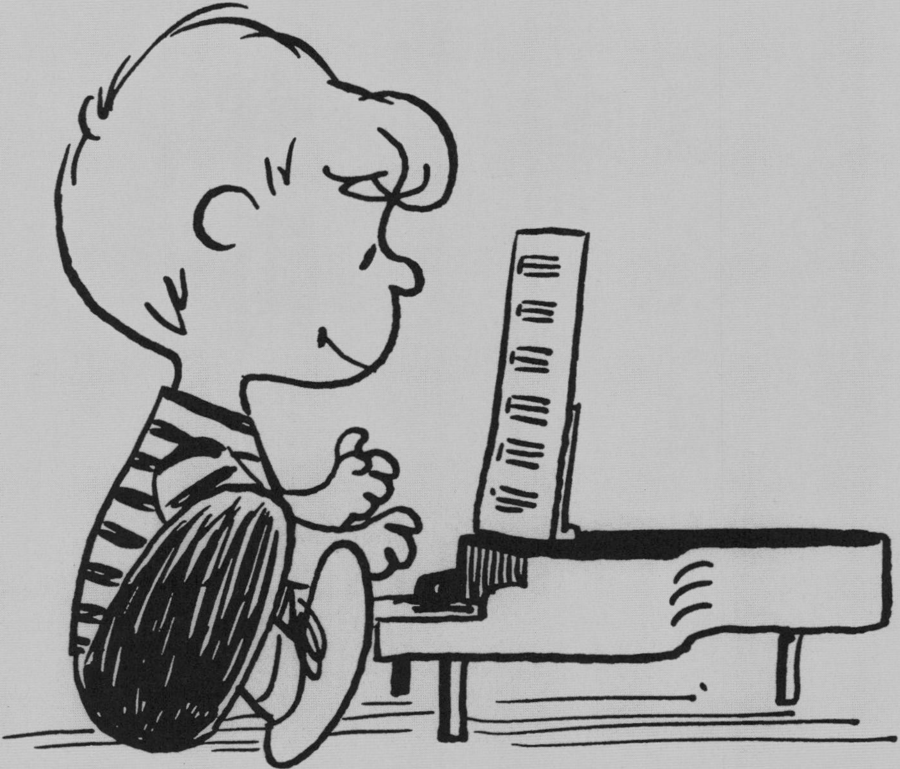

Security
is having
the music
in front
of you.

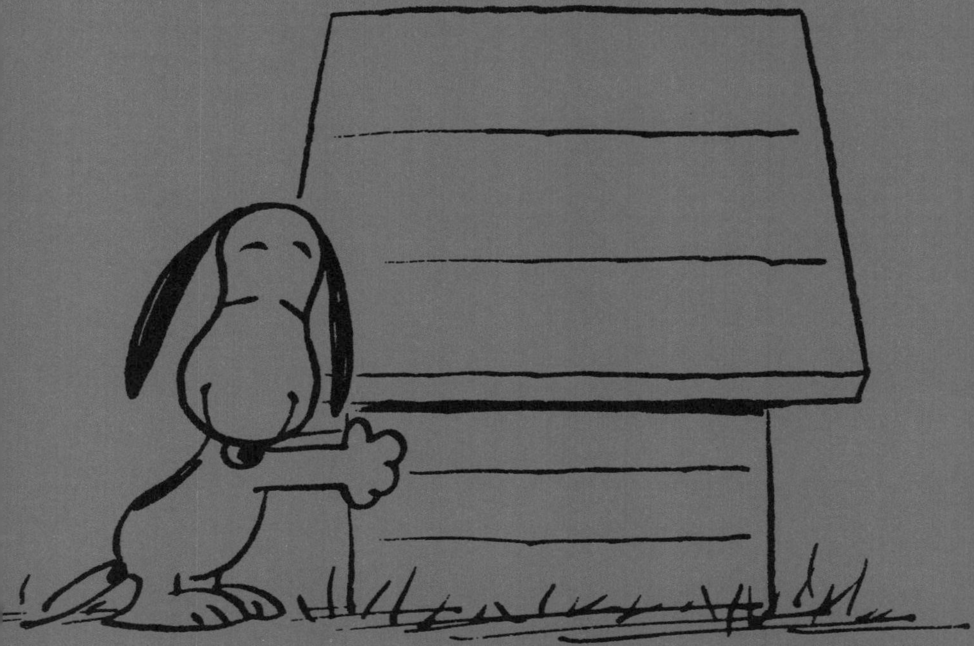

Security is where we call home.

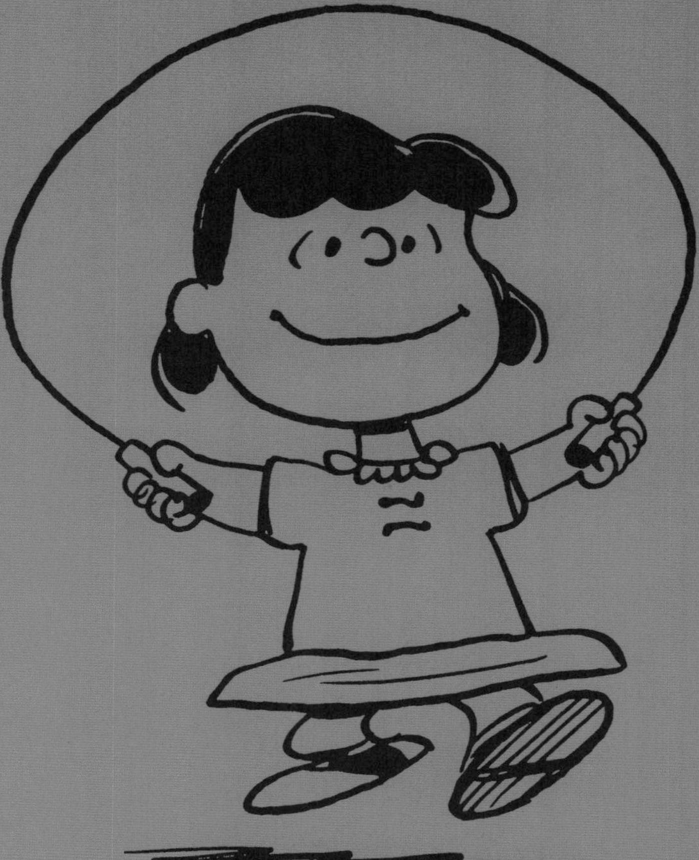

**Security
is knowing
you still have
quite a few
years to go.**

Security is having your socks match.

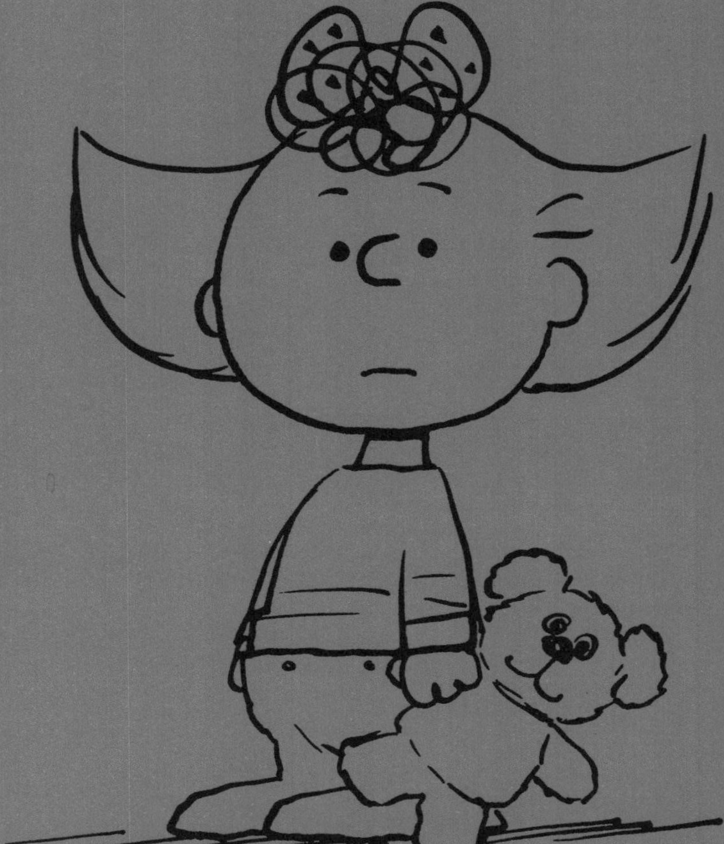

Security is knowing who the baby sitter is.

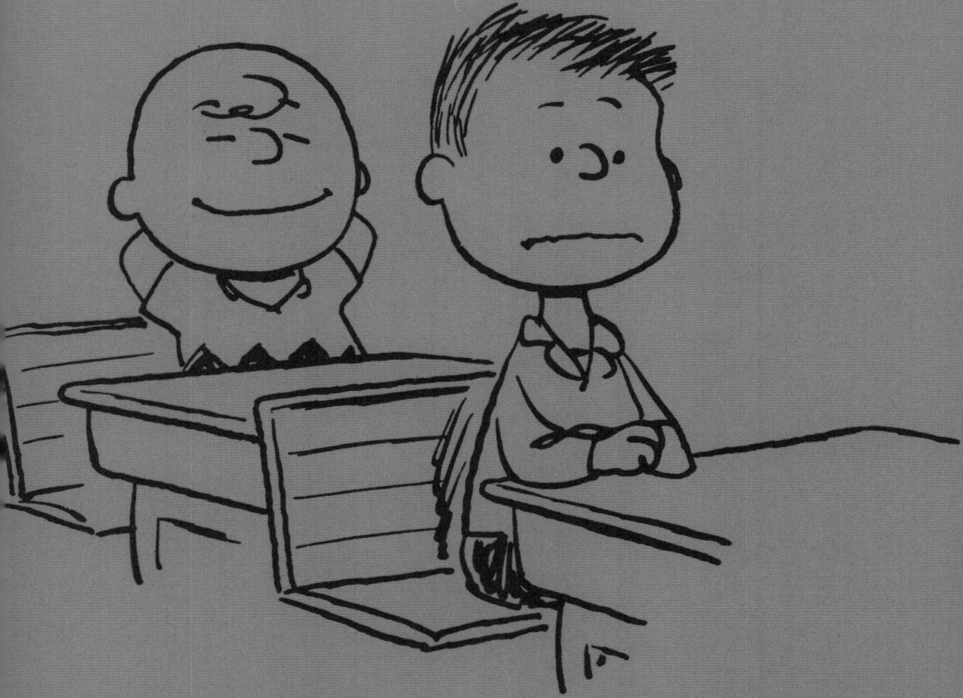

**Security
is knowing
you won't be
called on
to recite.**

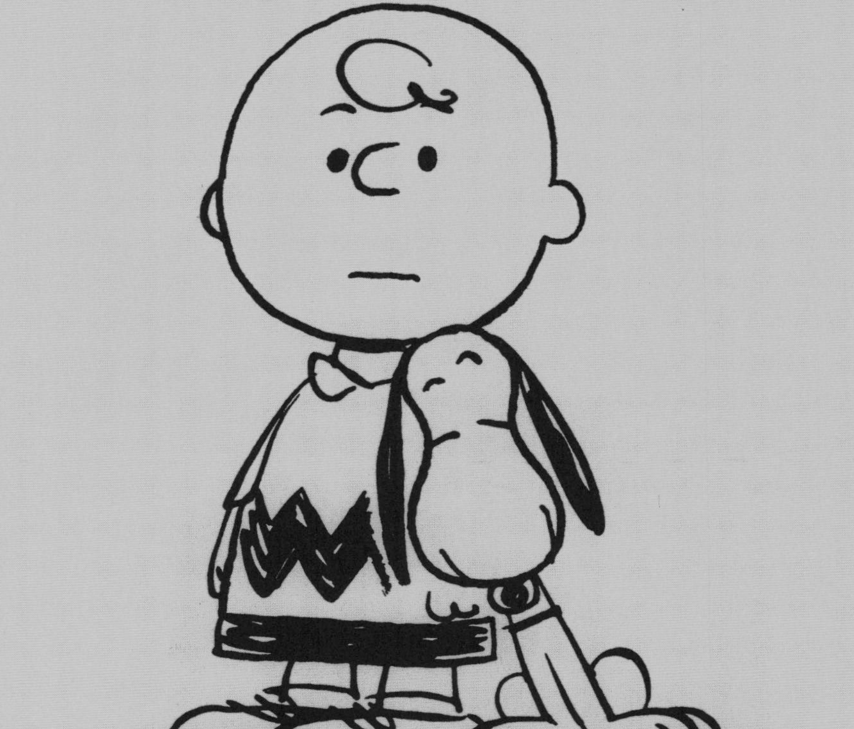

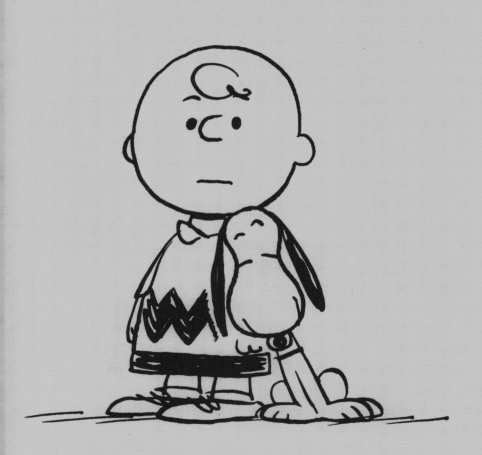

**Security
is having
someone
to lean
on.**

SECURITY IS A THUMB AND A BLANKET

PENGUIN WORKSHOP
An imprint of Penguin Random House LLC, New York

This edition published by Penguin Workshop, an imprint of Penguin Random House LLC, New York, 2022

PEANUTS and all related titles, logos and characters are trademarks of Peanuts Worldwide LLC

Visit us online at penguinrandomhouse.com.

Library of Congress Control Number: 2021043124

Manufactured in China

ISBN 9780593519516

10 9 8 7 6 5 4 3 2 TOPL

SECURITY IS A THUMB AND A BLANKET

BY

CHARLES M. SCHULZ

TO:

_____

FROM:

_____